Song *of* *the* Saints

CELEBRATING THE SAINTS WITH ANGLICAN PRAYER BEADS

Catherine Gotschall

Church
PUBLISHING

Unless otherwise noted, the Scripture quotations are from New Revised Standard Version Bible, copyright © 1989 National Council of the Churches of Christ in the United States of America. Used by permission. All rights reserved worldwide.

The Collects for each entry are drawn from the 1979 Book of Common Prayer.

Church Publishing
19 East 34th Street New York, NY 10016
www.churchpublishing.org

Cover design by David Baldeosingh Rotstein
Typeset by Andrew Berry

ISBN 978-1-64065-766-3 (paperback)
ISBN 978-1-64065-767-0 (eBook)

Library of Congress Control Number: 2025934365

CONTENTS

Introduction   1

A Brief History of Prayer Beads   6

How to Use Prayer Beads with the Prayers in This Book   12

THE SAINTS

ADVENT

1 Advent—Hildegard of Bingen   15

2 Advent—Anna Julia Haywood Cooper   19

3 Advent—Ambrose of Milan   23

4 Advent –Symeon the New Theologian   27

THE NATIVITY THROUGH THE EPIPHANY

The Nativity—Anselm of Canterbury   31

First Sunday after Christmas—Julian of Norwich   35

The Epiphany—Li Tim-Oi   39

ORDINARY TIME AFTER THE EPIPHANY

1 Epiphany—Polycarp   43

2 Epiphany—Charbel Makhlouf   46

3 Epiphany—Charles de Foucauld   50

4 Epiphany—Seraphim of Sarov   54

5 Epiphany—Frederick Douglass   58

6 Epiphany—Gregory of Nyssa   62

7 Epiphany—Toyohiko Kagawa   66

8 Epiphany—Perpetua and Felicity   70

Last Epiphany—Dietrich Bonhoeffer   74

LENT

1 Lent—Anthony of Egypt   78

2 Lent—Margaret of Cortona   81

3 Lent—Padre Pio   85

4 Lent—Sor Juana Inés de la Cruz   89

5 Lent—Mary of Egypt   93

PALM SUNDAY THROUGH TRINITY SUNDAY

Palm Sunday—Damien of Molokai   97

Easter—Óscar Romero   101

2 Easter—Maria Skobtsova of Paris   105

3 Easter—Mechthild of Hackeborn   109

4 Easter—Sojourner Truth   112

5 Easter—George Herbert   116

6 Easter—Hadewijch of Brabant   120

7 Easter—Anthony of Padua   123

Pentecost—Sundar Singh   127

Trinity Sunday—Athanasius of Alexandria   131

ORDINARY TIME AFTER PENTECOST

Proper 1—Louise de Marillac   135

Proper 2—Patrick of Ireland   139

Proper 3—Alcuin of York   143

Proper 4—Francis of Assisi   146

Proper 5—Charles Wesley   150

Proper 6—Catherine of Sienna   154

Proper 7—Sophrony of Essex   158

Proper 8—Marie of the Incarnation   162

Proper 9—Mary MacKillop   166

Proper 10—Benedict of Nursia   170

Proper 11—Teresa of Los Andes 174

Proper 12—Janani Luwum 178

Proper 13—Gregory the Great 182

Proper 14—Jonathan Myrick Daniels 186

Proper 15—Thomas à Kempis 190

Proper 16—Henry Budd 194

Proper 17—Bernard of Clairvaux 198

Proper 18—Edith Stein 202

Proper 19—Gertrude the Great 206

Proper 20—Thérèse of Lisieux 210

Proper 21—Teresa of Ávila 214

Proper 22—Faustina Kowalska 218

Proper 23—Bonaventure 222

Proper 24—Isaac the Syrian 225

Proper 25—Pauli Murray 228

Proper 26—Teresa of Kolkata 232

Proper 27—C. S. Lewis 236

Proper 28—Jerome 240

Proper 29—Thomas Merton 243

Next Steps 247

Acknowledgments 249

INTRODUCTION

"*I* sing a song of the saints of God," begins a well-loved hymn, but who are the saints and why do we sing their praises? How can they help us to deepen our faith? How can they bring us closer to God?

Most of us know something *about* the saints. Maybe you remember a story from Sunday School about Saint Francis and his love for animals, or perhaps you dressed up as Joan of Arc for an All Saints' Day pageant at church. Maybe you remember stories of healings or other miracles. But do you really *know* them? Think of Jesus—there's a big difference between knowing *about* Jesus and *knowing* Jesus.

When you know *about* someone, you relate to them primarily through your intellect, but when you *know* them—when you *really* know them—you relate to them through your heart.

Which begs the question, *how* do we come to know someone? Or something? Take, for example, a rose. How do we know what a rose is? We can read that a rose is a perennial flowering shrub with alternate leaves having serrated margins. We can further learn that the rose, in its wild form, has five light pink petals. But, reading a botanical description doesn't convey the essence of what a rose really is. For that, we need a personal encounter with a rose—we need to behold a rose, marvel at its glorious colors, touch its soft petals, breathe in its sweet fragrance.

What is true for roses is true for the saints. We can read books about the lives of the Jesus and the saints, but *real* knowledge and *real spiritual* growth happens in the context of *relationship,* through personal encounter. In our Christian faith, a key pathway for personal encounter with God—or with the saints—is through prayer. This book provides opportunities for personal encounters—through prayer—with sixty saints.

When I use the word "saint," I mean someone who has led a sacramental life; someone whose life and works are an outward and visible sign of deep and abiding inner spiritual grace. The saints I have chosen for this book demonstrate the Holy Spirit working through the lives of Christians across time and in every inhabited continent. They include holy men and women who have lived in every century of the common era from the first to the twentieth, and represent Roman Catholic, Orthodox, and Protestant traditions. Pope John Paul II often said that the Church has two lungs—East and West—and it must learn to breathe using both of them. Although the process for gaining official recognition as a saint varies across the churches, the saints in this book are all officially recognized by one of the Christian traditions with an official feast or commemoration day.

In writing *Song of the Saints,* I have especially enjoyed encountering saints from outside my own Anglican tradition. Coming to know saints from other Christian traditions has enlivened my own faith and deepened my spiritual practice. It is my hope that the words of these saints will be a blessing to you, as well, even (and perhaps especially) if they come from outside your Christian tradition. Some may object to the use of the word "saint" for someone whom their own church has not officially recognized; some Protestants may take issue with calling anyone a "saint." I use the term "saints" because it is scriptural; the word "saints" appears at least forty times in the New Testament. We are all called into continual communion with the saints. But, if using the word "saint" is a stumbling block for you, feel free consider them as "holy exemplars" instead, or use whatever term allows you to enter more completely into their story. What's important about the saints isn't that we admire them, but that they lead us to a closer relationship with Jesus, to a closer imitation of Him.

In medieval times, men and women often prayed using a book of hours. These beautifully illuminated texts typically contained prayers, psalms, passages from the Gospels. The books were used by lay Christians who wanted to incorporate elements of monastic devotion into their private prayers. I like to think of *Song of the Saints* as a book of "weeks"—a devotional guide containing prayers, illustrations, and Scripture passages. For each week of the liturgical year, a saint has been selected whose life reflects the themes from the Sunday Bible readings used by most churches in North America and the United Kingdom. Additionally, for each week there is a prayer formed from a saint's own words, a selected a passage from that Sunday's designated Bible readings and a collect—a short prayer—from the Episcopal Book of Common Prayer that brings together the common themes from the Bible readings.

The heartbeat of this book is the words of the saints themselves, formed into "prayers" that have been gleaned from their letters, sermons, prayers, treatises, and *vitae*. Like their lives, the words of the saints are sacramental, facing both inward and outward. I call them prayers, because they are intended to be recited using "prayer beads," but more accurately, they are prayerful encounters with the saints.

By spending daily devotional time with a saint over the course of a week, and by offering your breath and voice to bring new life to their thoughts and words, it is my hope that you will develop a deeper and more personal relationship with each saint. I hope that through your participation in these prayers you will experience yourself as part of the body of Christ and the communion of saints in a new and more meaningful way; that the prayers will help you to move beyond merely knowing about the saints into encounters with them as personal guides for your spiritual journey. When we honor the saints, we honor the Lord whom they served and by whose grace they were able to lead holy lives that inspire our faith today. As you say each saint's prayer, let their faith be rekindled in your heart.

In corporate worship, we pray and praise with our voices and our bodies: We stand to sing and to hear the Gospel proclaimed, we kneel to confess our sins, and we sit to learn. Prayer beads help us bring the involvement of our body and voice to private devotion. The tactile sensation of the beads in our hands helps quiet our minds and open our hearts. Praying with beads helps us slow things down and sharpen our focus as we become more present to the divine.

Repetition is an important component of praying with beads, as our prayers deepen with each heartfelt iteration. The physical act of touching each bead while praying aloud unites body, mind, and spirit in unified devotion to God. The near universal use of some form of prayer beads or knotted ropes in Christianity and nearly all other major religions testifies to the effectiveness of this practice. "Soul and body united by God compel each other," declares the English spiritual director, Reginald Somerset Ward. As we pray with beads, our prayers become etched into our hearts.

To supplement the prayers, I have written a brief biography for each saint that provides cultural and historical context for their life. These accounts are brief spiritual biographies that focus as much on the saint's spiritual formation and discernment as on their accomplishments. In some of the saints' stories historical fact and legend are interpenetrated, because, like poetry, legend can hold great truth, helping us to understand their "true" virtue and holiness. Through these biographies I have tried to convey each saint's unique charism and show how they responded to God's call to holiness—a universal call that speaks to us still.

The saints included here have led lives of exemplary holiness, but exemplary doesn't mean perfect. Or easy. They faced the same struggles that we face today: some had difficult marriages, some were divorced; some grieved the deaths of children, some were orphaned; some were bullied or were victims of physical or sexual abuse; some had poor relationships with their bosses and religious superiors; some lived with chronic physical or mental illness; many struggled with their faith and experienced times of spiritual dryness; a few even committed crimes. But through their trials, the Holy Spirit shone forth in their lives with a luminosity that still brightens our paths today.

The saints I have included are those whose words have been preserved. It should be noted however, that this introduces an inherent bias that favors the educated, the powerful, and those who speak the language of the dominant culture. This bias tends to exclude women and those who historically were undereducated and excluded from the power structure. Indigenous preachers, whose sermons and teachings were given in their native language and not translated into the languages of the powerful, as well as people living in poverty and slavery, who did not have access to education or whose education was prohibited by law are less likely to be included. While I have tried to overcome these inherent biases, I acknowledge that these saints are not fully representative of the saints of God.

Finally, I have drawn an illustration of each saint. The illustrations are not icons, but are nevertheless intended as an aid to prayer. In these illustrations, I have tried to create images that convey aspects of the saint's inner life and their outward ministry. It is my hope that the illustrations will help draw you into a more personal relationship with the saints as you pray their words. Since I am not an artist, most of the illustrations are inspired by the work of other artists, ancient and contemporary, whose contributions are credited at the end of each biography.

The saints point us to God and invite us to cooperate generously with God's grace in our own lives. Knowing how the saints have walked in faith can help form who we are as contemporary Christians. But more than just understanding the roots of our spiritual family, the saints can provide ongoing fellowship and guidance; they can become trusted companions on our spiritual journeys. I hope that you will come to know the saints for who they are, as much as for what they did. I hope that, taken collectively, the entries for each saint will help you synchronize your prayer life with the rhythms of the liturgical year.

Pope Benedict XVI said that the saints are the true bearers of light within history, for they are men and women of faith, hope, and love. As we grow in our relationships with the saints, we marvel how God's love is revealed through their lives. We see God's loving plan for humanity and for the Church emerge from humble acts of charity, devotion, and obedience. Inspired by their words and lives, may we all become more faithful agents of God's love.

A BRIEF HISTORY OF
PRAYER BEADS

Beads and prayers are natural companions. Our English word "bead" comes from the Old English word *bede,* which meant "prayer" and the older proto-Germanic word *bidam* which meant "to entreat." The modern English verb bid, meaning to ask, and the German word *bitte,* meaning "please" also come from this same origin. But beads and praying go back much farther than Anglo-Saxon England.

The first human use of beads was for personal adornment—beads are thought to be humanity's most ancient form of jewelry. In a Moroccan cave, archaeologists recently discovered beads that were made by humans more than 140,000 years ago: the beads, made from snail shells, had been modified with stone tools. Shells of this same particular species of snail have been unearthed in archaeological sites across North Africa, indicating cultural continuity among the human populations. In fact, archaeologists consider the distributed presence of these shells to be the first direct material evidence of modern social behavior, and are indicative of a widespread system of human communication. Beads are an important marker of the development of human civilization.

The use of beads for religious purposes is believed to have originated on the Indian subcontinent around the eighth century BCE. The first prayer "beads" were probably collections of pebbles or seeds that would be transferred from one bowl or pouch to another to count the 108 recitations of mantras or the various names of a deity, such as Krishna. For Hindus, the number 108 represents the wholeness of creation; it is also the number of the Upanishads, sacred Hindi texts. By using pre-counted stones, the worshiper could avoid the distraction of counting the number of repetitions and enter more deeply into the experience of prayer and devotion.

Eventually, whether through an adaptation of this practice or through finding a new purpose for beaded jewelry, strung beads became used as an aid to prayer. Hindus made circular bead chains, called *mala,* the Sanskrit word for garland, containing 108 beads of a similar size and a larger, uncounted "guru bead." There are sandstone representations of worshipers and deities holding *mala* dating from 185 BCE.

The number 108 is also sacred in Buddhism, and the use of prayer beads was adopted by Buddhist practitioners. A sacred Buddhist sutra from the fourth century BCE tells of a king who prayed to the Buddha for guidance in teaching his people. The Buddha told him. "King, if you want to eliminate earthly desires and put an end to their suffering, make a circular string of 108 beads made from the seeds of the Mokugenji tree. Recite *'Namu Buddha. Namu Dharma. Namu Sangha.'* Count one bead with each recitation." The use of prayer beads was also adopted by Jainists and Sikhs.

The first depiction of prayer beads in Western art may be a fresco dating to around 1600 BCE found on the Aegean island of Santorini. The image depicts the three female "adorants," or worshipers, near the altar of a sanctuary; one of the women holds a string of beads on her left hand. Another fresco from the same building depicts frolicking monkeys, which primatologists have recently identified as gray langurs, a species found only in India, suggesting the possibility of trade between the Greek islands and India. It is inviting to think that trade between these two regions helped to spread the use of prayer beads from India to the West.

Within the Christian tradition, the use of prayer beads—and their functional cousin, prayer ropes—dates to the Desert Fathers and Mothers in the third century. Saint Paul of Thebes (ca. 227–341), regarded as the first Egyptian hermit, would place 300 pebbles in his lap, as counters, and remove one with each repetition of prayer.

Shortly before his death, Paul of Thebes was visited by Saint Anthony the Great, who learned in a dream where to find the aged hermit. According to legend, Saint Anthony (though some claim it was Saint Pachomius) improved on Paul's method by using a cord with a series of knots tied along its length to count the number of prayers he recited. The great saint would tie one knot in a leather rope for every *Kyrie eleison* that he recited, but during the night, the devil would come and untie the knots to disrupt his count. One night, an angel appeared to Anthony (some versions of the legend claim that it was the Virgin Mary), and taught him a method of tying the knots so that each knot contained seven small crosses within it, rendering the devil powerless to negate the sign of the cross. To this day, Orthodox prayer ropes are still made using this complex knot, typically containing 33, 50, 100, or 150 knots, though even longer lengths are sometimes used. Orthodoxy considers the prayer rope, with a recitation of the Jesus Prayer for each knot, to be the "sword of the Spirit" (Eph. 6:17) because heartfelt prayer is a weapon to vanquish the devil.

The next important step in the use of beads as aids to Christian worship was the development of "paternoster" beads, strings of beads of various lengths, typically with a tassel or religious pendant at one end. The beads get their name from the opening words of the Lord's Prayer in Latin: *Pater Noster.* Worshipers, especially penitents, would use the strings of beads to count how many "Our Fathers" they recited. The beads were a sort of proto-rosary and were widely used in England and northern Europe in the early Middle Ages. Saint Gertrude, Abbess of Nivelles, who died in 659, is reported to have been buried with her prayer beads.

The first written reference to paternoster beads in England is found in the will of Lady Godiva (yes, that Lady Godiva, though her naked horseback romp through the streets of Coventry is a legend). Lady Godiva, whose name means "God's Gift," and her husband Leofric (the Grim), Earl of Mercia, were generous benefactors of the Church who founded several monasteries and chapels. Lady Godiva (or *Godgifu*) was the only woman listed as a major landholder following the Norman Conquest of 1066. She died shortly after the invasion and her will describes her "circle of prayer stones put on a thread in order that, by touching each one, she began each of her prayers and might not lose count of their number." She bequeathed this paternoster to a statue of the Blessed Virgin at the monastery in Coventry.

The use of paternoster beads continued to spread with the rise of the Cistercian and Carthusian orders in the eleventh and twelfth centuries. The lay brothers, who were often unable to read Latin psalters, were allowed to substitute the recitation of 150 *Pater Nosters* for praying the 150 psalms. In fact, the paternoster beads were sometimes called "the poor man's breviary." This practice gradually spread to the private devotions of the laity, especially in England: by the twelfth century, the Church encouraged the daily recitation of 150 Pater Nosters, often divided into three groups of fifty.

Prayer beads, along with the rising popularity of books of hours contributed greatly to the growth of private devotion as a supplement to corporate worship. Although the beads were called paternosters, they were used by the faithful for other devotions in addition to the Lord's Prayer. The varying number of beads on a string allowed people to choose their own forms of prayer and to customize their devotions to meet various needs. In Chaucer's *Canterbury Tales* (ca. 1390), he describes the Prioress as wearing a "pair of bedes" made of coral.

By the fourteenth and fifteenth centuries, paternosters had become so popular that many cathedrals had artisan bead makers, called "paternosterers," selling their wares from shops adjacent to church grounds. In fact, Newgate Market, next to St. Paul's Cathedral in London, was called Paternoster Square until 1872. Archaeological excavations in this area have turned up fragments indicating that the beads manufactured there were made of amber, boxwood, coral, bone, and jet, a type of fossilized wood; although glass, stone, and metal beads were sometimes used. In Paris, the paternoster guild had three separate divisions: one for bone and horn,

Funerary brass depicting a monk with paternoster beads from a London church, c. 1465.

one for coral and mother of pearl, and one for amber and jet. It is significant, I believe, that the beads were made from materials derived from living organisms, further linking the prayers from the created world with the Creator.

Parallel to the development and use of 150-bead paternosters was the evolution of the *Ave Maria* or "Hail Mary" prayer and its association with the paternoster practice. The first two phrases of the Hail Mary ("Hail Mary, full of grace, the Lord is with you," and, "Blessed are you among women, and blessed is the fruit of your womb"), both from Luke's Gospel, were linked together by Coptic Christians as early as 600. But it was not until 1568 that the Angelic Salutation and Elizabeth's salutation were linked with the final petition ("Holy Mary, Mother of God, pray for us sinners, now and at the hour of our death. Amen.") and officially adopted by the Council of Trent for inclusion in the Roman Breviary.

The devotion of the Holy Rosary also evolved in parallel with the development of the Hail Mary. Between the tenth and fifteenth centuries, it was not uncommon for private devotions to include groups of ten Hail Marys and one Our Father, using strings of beads as an aid to prayer. According to legend, in 1214, Saint Dominic (1172–1221), founder of the Dominican Order, was told by the Blessed Virgin to use the rosary as an aid to convert the Cathars. In 1520, Pope Leo X gave the Holy Rosary the official approbation of the Roman Catholic Church.

The use of prayer ropes to count recitations of the Jesus Prayer has been used by Orthodox Christians since the time of the Desert Fathers and Mothers. Devotion to the rosary has continued to grow in the Roman Catholic Church and remains an important and beloved practice. In the Anglican and Lutheran traditions, devotion to the rosary survived, but its use declined significantly. (Lutherans do not include the final petition to Mary.) It was not until the late twentieth century that these Christian traditions began to revive the use of prayer beads; soon other Protestant traditions followed suit, as well.

In the 1980s, a small group of Episcopalians in Texas developed the Anglican rosary as an aid to prayer. They retained the circular arrangement of large and small beads from the Holy Rosary, but reduced the number of beads to thirty-three: one for each year of the life of Christ. Instead of the "decades," or groups of ten beads found in the Holy Rosary, they adopted "weeks," groups of seven beads, acknowledging the number seven as the biblical number symbolizing completion. The arrangement and names for the beads are described more fully in the following section. Protestant prayer beads use the same configuration, but with the addition of a "resurrection" bead. All of the prayers in this book can be used with Anglican or Protestant prayer beads.

HOW TO USE PRAYER BEADS
WITH THE PRAYERS IN THIS BOOK

*N*ow that you've learned about the history of prayer beads, let's learn how to pray using Anglican prayer beads and explore the format of the prayers presented in this book. We'll use the prayer for Saint Seraphim of Sarov, found on page 54, to illustrate how the beads and the words of the prayers go together. If you're already familiar with prayer beads, you may want to skip this section.

Symbols used for the prayers in this book:

✟ Cross

O Invitatory Bead

    Φ Cruciform Bead

    • Weeks Bead

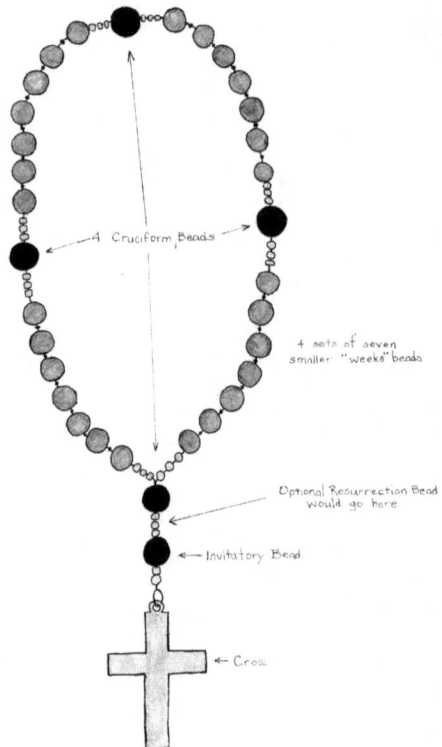

4 Cruciform Beads

4 sets of seven smaller "weeks" beads

Optional Resurrection Bead would go here

Invitatory Bead

Cross

Start by holding the cross between your thumb and first finger, and say:

☦ *The true aim of our Christian life is to acquire the Holy Spirit of God.*

Now, move your fingers to the invitatory bead, saying:

⭕ *The Holy Spirit dwells mystically in the hearts of those who believe in our Lord God and Savior Jesus Christ.*

Note: If your bead set includes a Resurrection bead, you may either skip this bead or, as I prefer, take a moment of silence to breathe deeply and rest in the presence of God.

The next bead is the first cruciform bead. Gently hold this bead and say:

✞ *The grace of God's Holy Spirit appears in light inexpressible to all to whom God reveals its power.*

Move to the first of the "weeks" beads and say:

• *The grace of the Holy Spirit is my lamp and light.*

Repeat this line six more times, moving along one bead with each repetition. Now, move to the second cruciform bead and say:

✞ *The more the heavenly riches of God's grace are given away, the more they increase in the giver.*

Move to the weeks beads and repeat the next line of the prayer seven times, advancing one bead with each repetition:

• *The Holy Spirit guides our steps into the way of peace.*

Move to the third cruciform bead and say:

✞ *The Lord seeks a heart that is filled with love of God and neighbor.*

Moving to the next set of weeks beads, repeat seven times, advancing one bead with each repetition:

• *Only good deeds done for Christ's sake bring us the fruits of the Holy Spirit.*

At the fourth cruciform bead, say:

✞ *In prayer we are granted to converse with our all-gracious and life-giving God and Savior.*

When you get to the last set of weeks beads, repeat the following line seven times, advancing one bead each time:

- *Great is the power of prayer; it brings the Spirit of God.*

  Complete the circle by advancing to the next cruciform bead and say:

✤ *When the mind and the heart are united in prayer, you feel that spiritual warmth which comes from Christ and fills the whole inner being with joy and peace.*

  Now leave the circle, returning to the invitatory bead and say:

○ *True enlightenment from the Lord is sent into the hearts of all who hunger and thirst for God's truth.*

  Finally, return to your cross bead and say the final line of the prayer:

✝ *The Spirit of God reminds us of the words of our Lord Jesus Christ, gladden our hearts and guiding our steps into the way of peace.*

This same format of recitation and repetition is used for all of the prayers in this book. Repeat this pattern for all of the saints, as you come to know them by giving your voice to their words. Remember: always begin and end with the cross.

We give thanks to the Father, who has made us worthy to share in the inheritance of the saints in light.

—Colossians 1:12

HILDEGARD OF BINGEN

Mystic, Monastic, and Theologian (born ca. 1098–died 1179)

Let us then lay aside the works of darkness and put on the armor of light.

—Romans 13:12

☩ O sweet Divinity and O lovely Life, in Whom I may put on a robe of glory, I long for You.

O Let everyone who understands God by faith, with joyful devotion sing to Him without ceasing.

☩ The song of rejoicing tells of the glory of Heaven, and lifts on high what the Word has shown.

• The song of rejoicing summons the Holy Spirit.

☩ The Good Shepherd has brought back to the fold with joy the sheep that was lost.

• The people who fell into sin return by God's will to repentance.

☩ Offer praises unceasingly with heart and mouth to the Supernal Creator.

• Adore and love God with simple mind and pure devotion.

☩ The wonders of God are enveloped for you in a sweet and delightful song.

• The Word is the sacred sound to which all creation resounds.

☩ The power of God is everywhere and encompasses all things.

O Let every spirit who wills to believe in God, praise the Lord, Him Who is the Lord of all.

☩ Praise God, ye blessed hearts, for the beauty of the Most High.

Almighty God, give us grace to cast away the works of darkness, and put on the armor of light, now in the time of this mortal life in which your Son Jesus Christ came to visit us in great humility; that in the last day, when he shall come again in his glorious majesty to judge both the living and the dead, we may rise to the life immortal; through him who lives and reigns with you and the Holy Spirit, one God, now and for ever. *Amen.*

Hildegard was a theologian, poet, composer, physician, naturalist, and abbess whose vivid originality and holiness continue to enlighten the Church today.

The tenth child born to a wealthy family in 1098, Hildegard was promised to the Church as a tithe. At the age of eight, she was consigned to the care of Jutta of Sponheim, abbess of a nearby Benedictine convent, where Hildegard was received as an oblate. There, Hildegard and Jutta lived as anchorites, walled in to a small room, able to communicate with the world only through a small window opening. Hildegard made her religious profession in 1115.

After Jutta's death in 1136, Hildegard assumed leadership of the convent at Disibodenberg, which flourished under her spiritual direction. In 1150, Hildegard and twenty sisters founded a new monastery in Rupertsberg, near Bingen. Fifteen years later, Hildegard established a second convent in nearby Eibingen, serving as abbess of both religious communities.

Starting at the age of five, and continuing into adulthood, the Lord endowed Hildegard with mystical visions, which were often followed by intense pain, illness, and periods of incapacity. Later, Hildegard dictated an account of her visions to the monk Volmar, who served as her amanuensis and secretary. Hildegard also wrote letters to Bernard of Clairvaux and

Pope Eugene III describing these visions, receiving confirmation of their authenticity.

The visions of Hildegard are recorded in *Scito Vias Domini,* ("Know the Ways of the Lord," usually shortened to *Scivias),* completed in 1151, and two other related works. These works describe and interpret her thirty-five visions that revealed to her the nature of the cosmos, the mysterious marriage of God and humanity through the incarnation of Christ, and the meaning of the Trinity. When Hildegard was in her seventies, she commissioned an illuminated manuscript to accompany the text of *Scivias.* Although the original was lost in the bombing of Dresden in 1945, a facsimile copy, made by the nuns of Eibingen in 1920, still exists.

Hildegard, known as the "Sibyl of the Rhine," was the most prolific composer of the Middle Ages—male or female—having written the words and music for nearly eighty compositions. She was the first Western composer to have a clearly recognizable musical voice. Her melismatic sacred compositions, most of which were written between 1151 and 1158, were intended to be sung by the nuns at Rupertsberg. Her liturgical drama *Ordo Virtutum* is the first known morality play and the only medieval musical drama for which attributions of music and text have survived.

Hildegard saw life's creative power as a sustaining force and an expression of the divine healing power in all things, which she called *viriditas.* She was a skilled observer of nature and wrote of the healing powers of plants, animals, and crystals, compiling a medical compendium of remedies, *Causae et Curae.*

When Hildegard died in 1179 in the abbey in Rupertsberg at the age of eighty-one, the nuns at her deathbed saw two streams of light from the heavens enter the room where she lay.

Hildegard was the first great female theologian to be named a Doctor of the Church, as decreed by Pope Benedict XVI in 2012, calling her as "authentic teacher of theology and a profound scholar of natural science and music."

Hildegard is celebrated on September 12 by the Anglican Communion, the Lutheran Church and the Roman Catholic Church.

First Week of Advent

This prayer is taken from the thirteenth vision of Book III of *Scivias* and from her letter to Bernard of Clairvaux. This illustration was drawn from a print in an eighteenth-century botanical encyclopedia. The scroll that she is holding reads, *Sci Vias Domini,* the title of her major work.

ANNA JULIA HAYWOOD COOPER

Educator (1858/9–1964)

He shall not judge by what his eyes see, or decide by what his ears hear; but with righteousness he shall judge the poor, and decide with equity for the meek of the earth.

—Isaiah 11:3–4

✠ One needs occasionally to stand aside from the hum and rush of human interests and passions to hear the voices of God.

○ The image of God in human form, whether in marble or in clay, in alabaster or in ebony, is consecrated and inviolable.

✠ Jesus believed in the infinite possibilities of an individual soul. His faith was a triumphant realization of the eternal development of the best in man.

• Faith means treating the truth as true.

✠ A nation enamored of the ideal of the Rights of Man could not rest indifferent in the face of the idea of slavery.

• The divine Spark is capable of awakening at the most unexpected moment.

✠ The quiet face of Jesus is ever seen a little way ahead, never too far to come down to and touch the life of the lowest in the darkest days, yet ever leading onward, still onward.

• The evolution of civilization is His care; eternal progress, His delight.

✠ In the universe of God, nothing is trivial or mean; and the recognition it seeks is not through the survival of the bullies but through the universal application of the Golden Rule.

• We have a destiny to fulfill, we "must be about our Father's business."

✠ We can paint what is true with the calm spirit of those who know their cause is right and who believe there is a God who judgeth the nations.

○ Not till we hear the angels' voices audibly saying "Come, let us depart hence," shall we cease to believe and cling to the promise, "I am with you to the end of the world."

✠ May God protect and bless your courageous designs.

Second Week of Advent

Merciful God, who sent your messengers the prophets to preach repentance and prepare the way for our salvation: Give us grace to heed
their warnings and forsake our sins, that we may greet with joy the
coming of Jesus Christ our Redeemer; who lives and reigns with you
and the Holy Spirit, one God, now and for ever. *Amen.*

Anna Julia Haywood Cooper used her keen intellect, unwavering moral
compass, and passion for education to serve God by advocating for
the rights of women and men of all races.

The child of Hannah Stanley Haywood, an enslaved woman, and an un-
named White man, Anna Haywood was born into slavery in Raleigh, North
Carolina, in 1858. At the age of nine, she received a scholarship to attend St.
Augustine's Normal School and Collegiate Institute, a school founded by the
Episcopal Church to educate formerly enslaved Americans of African descent
and prepare them for careers in teaching or ministry.

At the school, she successfully advocated that girls be allowed to study
Greek, Latin, and algebra, rather than the standard "home economics" curriculum. While attending the school Anna became an Episcopalian; when she was
nineteen, she married George Cooper, the second African American ordained
to the Episcopal clergy.

Following her husband's death two years later, Anna devoted her life to
education and the pursuit of social justice. In 1881, she was awarded a full
scholarship to attend Oberlin College. There, she broke down gender-related
barriers, convincing the school's administration to allow her to take the more
rigorous "gentleman's" curriculum. After earning her bachelor's and master's
degrees in mathematics from Oberlin, she became a teacher of math and
science at the M Street High School, in Washington, DC. While working

as a teacher at the M Street School, Anna wrote *A Voice from the South by a Black Woman of the South,* a collection of essays published in 1902 that articulates the interactions of race, gender, and class. This landmark volume called for education of Blacks and women, which she saw as a God-given right, rebuking "the weak-eyed Christians who cannot read the Golden Rule across the color line."

It was also in 1902 that Anna was appointed principal of the M Street School. In this role, she worked to shift the focus of the school's offerings away from vocational training to a more demanding college-preparatory training. Although her students earned acceptance at Harvard, Yale, and Brown Universities, the school's board recommended that she discontinue the nonvocational approach that she had championed. When Anna refused to abandon the more rigorous curriculum, the board forced her to resign in 1906.

Following her dismissal, Anna took a job teaching languages at a school in Missouri while she legally challenged the board's actions. After four years, her challenged proved successful and she was rehired by the M Street School, but as a teacher of Latin, rather than as principal. She remained in this position for the next twenty years, but spent her summers from 1911 to 1913 in France, where she studied literature, linguistics, and French history.

In 1914, Anna was accepted into the doctoral program at Columbia University in New York, where she completed her coursework requirements while working full time as a teacher. At this time, she also adopted her late nephew's five orphaned children, all under the age of thirteen, and moved into a larger home to accommodate her expanded family. Unable to complete Columbia's residency requirements because of her new family responsibilities, Anna transferred to the Sorbonne in Paris, where at the age of sixty-six she became one of the first women of African descent to earn a PhD from the prestigious French university.

After she left the M Street School at the age of seventy-two, Anna served as president of Freylinghuysen University in Washington, DC, and later as its registrar. She died in 1964, having served God for 105 years.

Second Week of Advent

Anna Julia Haywood Cooper is commemorated in the Anglican Communion on February 28.

This prayer is taken from *A Voice from the South by a Black Woman of the South.*
This image is based on a drawing of "Mrs. Anna Cooper" that was published
on the cover of the March 26, 1904, issue of *The Colored American,* a weekly
newspaper published in Washington, DC.

AMBROSE OF MILAN

Bishop and Theologian (ca. 336–397)

A highway shall be there, and it shall be called the Holy Way; the unclean shall not travel on it, but it shall be for God's people; no traveler, not even fools, shall go astray.

—Isaiah 35:8

☦ All praise, eternal Son, to thee, whose advent sets Thy people free.

○ Let us not be ashamed to confess our sins unto the Lord.

✤ When the Lord forgave all sins, he made exception of none.

• Jesus, look upon those who lapse, and by Thy seeing us, correct us.

✤ If Thou lookest, our sins will fall away and our fault will be washed away by weeping.

• Wash my mind's every step, that I may not sin again.

✤ Shed through our hearts Thy piercing ray, our souls' dull slumber drive away.

• You are the light when all is dark.

✤ No one can repent to good purpose unless he hopes for mercy.

• Wash me with your tears, Lord Jesus.

✤ The same God that requires repentance promises forgiveness.

○ Come, that I may think no more on works of darkness but on works of light.

☦ Savior of the nations, come.

Stir up your power, O Lord, and with great might come among us; and, because we are sorely hindered by our sins, let your bountiful grace and mercy speedily help and deliver us; through Jesus Christ our Lord, to whom, with you and the Holy Spirit, be honor and glory, now and for ever. *Amen.*

Ambrose of Milan has been called the most talented bishop of the early church for his courage and fair-minded administration, establishing clear boundaries between church and state. He was also a gifted preacher and writer of hymns.

Ambrose was the son of a wealthy family; his father was a praetorian prefect in Gaul (now Trier, Germany); his mother was also highly regarded for her considerable intellect. According to legend, when Ambrose was a baby, his father saw a swarm of bees land on his cradle, which he took as a sign that young Ambrose would grow to be a "honey-tongued" speaker. After his father's death, Ambrose's family removed to Rome, where Ambrose studied rhetoric and law, training for a career in government. He became a governor of Italy's northern provinces, which included the city of Milan, before he was thirty.

When the bishop of Milan, an Arian proponent, died in 374, Ambrose was called to oversee the election of the new bishop. During a raucous meeting where Arians and Orthodox Christians vied for power, someone in the crowd shouted "Ambrose for bishop!" Soon the entire crowd echoed the chant. Initially, Ambrose declined the position (although he was raised in a Christian family, he had never been baptized). The Roman emperor Valentinian, however, would not take no for an answer. Bowing to popular demand, he placed Ambrose under arrest until he agreed to serve. The saint ultimately complied. One month after his baptism, Ambrose was consecrated bishop of Milan. On becoming bishop, he gave his property to the poor and diligently studied Holy Scripture and Christian theology.

Ambrose was a strong defender of church orthodoxy against heresy, but his greatest contribution to the church may have been clarifying the separate roles of church and state. He helped establish the concept of the Christian ruler as a faithful leader "serving under orders of Christ," and thus subject to the strictures of his bishop.

During his episcopacy, Ambrose interacted with three different Roman emperors, but he's most closely associated with Theodosius. After Theodosius ordered the massacre of thousands of Thessalonians in 390, in retribution for the death of a Roman official during a riot, Ambrose forbade him to enter the church or partake of the sacraments until he had publicly repented for this deed.

The sermons of Ambrose were held in such high esteem that Pelagius described him as "the flower of Latin eloquence." Such was his fame that young Augustine, then a professor of rhetoric and a skeptic of Christianity, came from Hippo to Milan to hear him preach. Four years later, Augustine was baptized by Ambrose, having become a convert to Christianity. It was Augustine who later persuaded Paulinus, secretary to Ambrose, to write his first biography, dated 422.

In addition to his brilliance in elocution, theology, and administration, Ambrose was also a writer of hymns; some of which are still sung today, including the Advent hymn, "Savior of the Nations, Come" ("*Veni Redemptor gentium*"). He is also credited with introducing many beautiful chants from the Eastern liturgy to the Western church. Six hymns attributed to Ambrose, along with nine others (collectively referred to as the Ambrosian hymns) formed the Old Hymnal used in the Ambrosian Rite of Milan. In his biography of Ambrose, Paulinus said, "Now for the first time, antiphons, hymns, and vigils began to be part of the observance of the church in Milan, which devout observance lasts to our day, not only in that church but in nearly every province of the West." Many attribute the importance of hymn singing in the Western liturgy to the influence of Ambrose.

Third Week of Advent

The feast day for Saint Ambrose is celebrated throughout the Church on December 7. His feast day is not the date of his death, as is typical for the saints, but the date of his consecration as bishop, honoring his contributions to church doctrine.

The words of this prayer are taken from the Ambrosian hymns, his essay *On Repentance,* and his letter to his sister. The illustration was inspired by an etching by Jacques Callot printed in 1636.

SYMEON THE NEW THEOLOGIAN

Poet, Monastic (ca. 949–1022)

Restore us, O Lord God of hosts; let your face shine, that we may be saved.

—Psalms 80:19

✠ Behold, Christ, my affliction, behold my faintheartedness, behold my powerlessness and have pity on me, O Logos!

O Shine on me now, as of old, and illuminate my soul, enlighten my eyes to see You, the light of the world.

✠ Tear out the roots of wickedness and evil from the depths, my Christ, and purify my soul.

• Light the lamp of my soul before it grows dark.

✠ I shout to you asking to be purified anew and to enjoy fully your light, now and always.

• If I were separated from the light, how should I flee the darkness?

✠ You chase out the gloom of my sins and you cleanse the shame of my heart.

• You make me a light, I who was darkened.

✠ You give me your incorruptible purity, O Logos!

• You are a light that knows no evening; a sun that never sets.

✠ Love is the divine Spirit, the light that illuminates all things.

O You shine around me with a ray of immortality and I am both stupefied and burning within.

✠ Receive me as the least of your hired servants that I may serve You, my Savior, and receive your divine Spirit.

Purify our conscience, Almighty God, by your daily visitation, that your
Son Jesus Christ, at his coming, may find in us a mansion prepared for
himself; who lives and reigns with you, in the unity of the Holy Spirit,
one God, now and for ever. *Amen.*

Symeon the New Theologian, one of the most important poets and
spiritual writers of the Byzantine East, shares his experience and
direct knowledge of God's uncreated light in language that seems both ancient
and new.

Symeon was born in 949 in Asia Minor, near the modern city of Ankara,
Turkey. He was the son of a wealthy and noble Byzantine family who sent him
to be educated in Constantinople when he was about nine years old. There he
lived with his uncle who groomed him for a position in the Byzantine civil
service. When Symeon was fourteen, he met a holy monk named Symeon the
Devout (also known as Symeon the Studite) who agreed to provide spiritual
direction, but persuaded the younger Symeon to postpone monastic commitment until after he had completed a period of public service. In a work that
is believed to be autobiographical, Symeon describes himself as a young man
who was "polished in dress, appearance, and comportment," and yet he "threw
himself into the abyss" of a life filled with "dissipation and frivolity." At about
this time, Symeon experienced a profound ecstatic state, in which he saw God
as a living and radiant light and was instructed by Christ to surrender himself
to his spiritual father.

Through his mystical experiences, Symeon received the grace to amend his
ways, and at the age of twenty-seven, he entered the Monastery of Stoudion.
There he offered himself completely to the direction of the elder Symeon, who

guided the younger man in the life of prayer and asceticism. However, young Symeon's fervent zeal caused disruption within the monastery, and after about a year the abbot directed him to leave the community.

Symeon entered the smaller monastery of St. Mamas, a few miles away, though he remained under the spiritual direction of his mentor. Symeon took his monastic vows, was tonsured shortly after arriving at Mamas, and was soon ordained a priest. The monastery was in a state of disrepair and spiritual decline, so Symeon undertook the restoration of the half-ruined buildings; when the abbot died, around 980, he was elected as the new abbot. His efforts to raise the ascetic standards and to exhort the monks to greater discipline in prayer met considerable resistance. One morning, in about 997, a group of thirty monks rebelled against him and came at him "like enraged dogs," but Symeon, remaining calm and smiling, held his ground. The rebels then appealed to the Patriarch of Constantinople to have him removed, but were denied and later were expelled. Symeon continued as abbot for ten more years, exhorting his monks to high levels of sanctity and contemplation, finally resigning his position in 1005, after a tenure of twenty-five years.

The retired abbot remained active, providing advice and spiritual direction to many followers. In 1009, however, a conflict arose between Symeon and a religious advisor to the Patriarch, regarding matters of theology and liturgy. After a hearing, Symeon was exiled and he took up residence in a chapel on the other side of the Bosporus. Although Symeon's exile was later lifted, he saw his exile as a way of sharing in the sufferings of Christ, and lived out his exile peacefully and without bitterness. It was here that Symeon composed many of his hymns, noted for their radiance and emotive style.

He left a substantial body of work, including hymns, catechetical treatises, and spiritual exercises that laid the foundation for the Eastern tradition of hesychastic mysticism. Symeon died in 1022. Many consider him to be the most important Byzantine religious thinker between John of Damascus (ca. 675–749) and Gregory Palmas (1296–1357).

Although the date of his death was March 12, the feast day for Symeon the New Theologian is often celebrated by the Orthodox Church on October 12 to avoid conflict with Lent.

This prayer was taken from the hymns of Saint Symeon. The name of the artist who first painted the icon of Saint Symeon the New Theologian that inspired this illustration has been lost to history, but his work lives on, as the painting has become the most frequently used image of the saint in contemporary usage.

ANSELM OF CANTERBURY

Archbishop of Canterbury,
Doctor of the Church (ca. 1033–1109)

For the grace of God has appeared, bringing salvation to all, training us to renounce impiety and worldly passions, and in the present age to live lives that are self-controlled, upright, and godly, while we wait for the blessed hope and the manifestation of the glory of our great God and Savior, Jesus Christ.

—Titus 2:11–13

☩ O Lord my God, Teach my heart where and how to seek you, where and how to find you.

○ I pray that I may so know you and love you that I may rejoice in you.

✤ Your joy fills my whole heart, mind, and soul, yet joy beyond measure still remains.

• I have found a fullness of joy that is more than full.

✤ Your blessed ones will rejoice as much as they love, and they will love as much as they know.

• Let the knowledge of you increase in me.

✤ Let me receive that which you promised through your truth.

• I pray that I may receive you.

✤ Speak, Lord, to your servant, in the depths of my heart.

• Let your love grow in me.

✤ God of truth, I ask that I may receive, so that my joy may be full.

○ Let my soul hunger for the fullness of joy, let my flesh thirst for it, and my whole being desire it.

☩ Until I enter into the joy of my Lord, who is God, one and triune, blessed forever. *Amen.*

The Nativity of the Lord

O God, you make us glad by the yearly festival of the birth of your only Son Jesus Christ: Grant that we, who joyfully receive him as our Redeemer, may with sure confidence behold him when he comes to be our Judge; who lives and reigns with you and the Holy Spirit, one God, now and for ever. *Amen.*

Although Anselm's motto was "Faith seeking understanding," it is his warm and heartfelt response to God that has transformed the faith of Christians for nearly a millennium.

Anselm was born in Aosta, in the foothills of the Italian Alps (then part of the Kingdom of Burgundy), in 1033. His parents, who were from noble families, provided Anselm with a sound classical education and taught him to love God. According to his biographer, Eadmer, Anselm had a vision as a young boy that he climbed to the summit of a nearby mountain, seeking Heaven. There he sat before the throne of God and conversed with the Lord and he was served bread of "exceeding whiteness." He later told his mother that he had eaten the Bread of God.

When Anselm was fifteen, he applied to enter a local monastery but was refused acceptance because his father opposed his religious vocation. At the age of twenty-three, he left home, crossing the Alps to live in Burgundy with his mother's family. He eventually made his way to the Bec monastery in Normandy, hoping to study with the abbot Lanfranc, considered to be the foremost teacher of his time.

At twenty-seven, Anselm began his novitiate at Bec and was made prior only three years later. Despite his young age, Anselm proved to be an able administrator and a loving mentor of young monks. Fifteen years later, in 1078, he was

The Nativity of the Lord

elected abbot. It was at Bec that Anselm wrote his *Monologion* and *Proslogion,* among his most famous and beloved writings. It was also at Bec that he wrote his *Prayers and Meditations,* as well as many letters of spiritual direction. With these works he introduced a new style of devotional writing, drawing readers into a warmer and more personal relationship with God and promoting service based on love, rather than ecclesiastical obligation.

Anselm was one of the first writers to refer to "our Lord, our Mother." As abbot of Bec, he increased both the spiritual standing of the abbey as well as its real estate holdings, obtaining land rights in England from William the Conqueror.

In England, the relationship between the monarchy and the church was becoming contentious. Lanfranc, the former abbot of Bec, became the Archbishop of Canterbury in 1078. After Lanfranc's death in 1089, King William II appropriated lands and revenues belonging to the church and refused to appoint a new archbishop. However, when William II was stricken with a grave illness, he repented of his actions and nominated Anselm as Archbishop of Canterbury.

At first Anselm declined, but later reluctantly acceded to the wishes of the British clerics, and after negotiating the restoration of the church's lands, he was consecrated in 1093. Such was his reluctance, that the archbishop's crozier was forcefully placed into his closed fist.

The conflicts between the Crown and the Church continued, however, and Anselm went into voluntary exile in France in 1097, rather than agreeing to the king's demands. During this time the pope wrote to the English king, threatening excommunication if Anselm was not allowed to exercise his office; King William did not reply and took no action.

With the accession of King Henry I to the English throne in 1100, Anselm returned from exile. However, new conflicts arose between the authorities of the Crown and the Church, prompting Anselm's second exile from 1103 to 1106. Eventually, a compromise was reached and Anselm returned to Canterbury, where he died in 1109. Many consider him to be the most significant theologian between Augustine and Thomas Aquinas, and the most influential of all the Archbishops of Canterbury. Anselm was proclaimed to be a Doctor of the Church in 1720 with the title "Magnificent Doctor."

Anselm is celebrated on April 21 by the Anglican Communion, the Lutheran Church, and the Roman Catholic Church.

> This prayer is taken from the final chapter of Anselm's *Proslogion* and from his *Prayers and Meditations*. The drawing reproduces a picture of an archbishop—presumably Anselm—from the copy of Anselm's *Prayers and Meditations* found in a twelfth-century illuminated text.

The Nativity of the Lord

JULIAN OF NORWICH

Mystic and Theologian (ca. 1342–after 1417)

It was fitting that God, for whom and through whom all things exist, in bringing many children to glory, should make the pioneer of their salvation perfect through sufferings.

—Hebrews 2:10

✢ God, of your goodness give me yourself, for you are enough for me.

O The greatest honor we can give Almighty God is to live gladly because of the knowledge of his love.

✤ God loved us before he made us; and his love has never diminished and never shall.

• Everything that is, has its being through the love of God;

✤ It is God's wish that we seek to behold him;

• God will graciously show himself to us.

✤ The simple enjoyment of our Lord is a most blessed form of thanksgiving;

• The fullness of joy is to behold God in everything.

✤ Our Lord is everything that is good and comforting and helpful.

• The soul can rest in nothing but in God.

✤ Because of the tender love which our good Lord feels for us, he supports us in our suffering;

O God safely protects us in both sorrow and joy equally.

✢ All shall be well, and all shall be well, and all manner of things shall be well.

Almighty God, you have poured upon us the new light of your incarnate Word: Grant that this light, enkindled in our hearts, may shine forth in our lives; through Jesus Christ our Lord, who lives and reigns with you, in the unity of the Holy Spirit, one God, now and for ever. *Amen.*

More than 650 years ago, Julian of Norwich saw the face of Christ. Her account of these revelations, the first book in the English language known to have been written by a woman, brings all of us face to face with the living Christ.

Little is known about Julian's life, but her book, *Revelations of Divine Love,* provides a few clues. Julian purposefully deflects attention away from herself and her life story, urging the reader not to pay "attention to the . . . sinful creature to whom this vision was shown," but to "eagerly, attentively, lovingly, and humbly contemplate God" through the visions that were given to her. Nevertheless, by considering her times, and piecing together clues from her writing, a picture of her life emerges.

Julian was born about the year 1342; it is believed that her father died when she was about six years old, during the first wave of the bubonic plague. She was raised in the faith, praying, while still a child, that God would grant her three "graces": to bear witness to the Passion of Christ, to endure a life-threatening illness, and to experience the three wounds of contrition, compassion, and longing for God. Based on her text, many scholars believe that Julian had been both a wife and a mother, and speculate that her husband and child died in the third wave of the bubonic plague, which struck Norwich in 1369.

Julian states that these revelations "were shown to a simple uneducated creature" in 1373, when she was "thirty and a half years old." She received the

First Sunday after Christmas

showings when she was near death from an unknown illness. The priest at her bedside administered last rites and held a crucifix before her eyes, urging her to gaze upon it. As she fixed her eyes on her crucified Lord, she experienced a series of sixteen visions, or "showings," as she called them, over a period of several days, while she recovered.

Four years after her visions, Julian became an "anchoress" at a church in Norwich, England, at that time a large city second in importance only to London. An anchoress (or "anchorite" for men, from the Greek word meaning "to withdraw") is someone who withdraws from the secular world in order to live a life of ascetic devotion. They lived in enclosed cells attached to a church called anchorholds. The cell typically had three windows: one into the church, so the anchoress could view the Mass and receive the Eucharist; a window to an adjoining room through which they received food and passed out "nightsoil" to an attendant; and a window to the outside world, where the faithful could come to seek their counsel. Julian entered her anchorhold in 1379 and lived there nearly forty years, until her death in 1418. Approximately five years before her death, Julian was visited by the pilgrim and mystic, Margery Kempe, who wrote about this visit in *The Book of Margery Kempe,* the first known autobiography in the English language.

Julian's *Revelations* exist in both a "short text" of twenty-five chapters written shortly after she received the visions, and a "long text" of eighty-six chapters written after some twenty years of further reflection on their meaning.

In her writing, Julian conveys her intimate and tender relationship with a God who loves humankind unconditionally, who "shows us our sin by the pure, sweet light of mercy and grace, without wrath or blame." Julian sees in God the qualities of both mother and father; she likens Christ's feeding us with his blood in the Eucharist to a mother feeding an infant with her milk. She also basks in the protection of a father who will "always keep you very safe." In one of her visions, Julian sees the whole of creation in the palm of her hand, "the size of a hazelnut," and realizes that it exists "and will last forever because...God made it, God loves it, and God takes care of it."

First Sunday after Christmas

Julian of Norwich is commemorated by the Anglican Communion on May 8.

This prayer was taken from both the short and long texts of *Revelations of Divine Love.* The illustration depicts Julian holding "a little thing the size of a hazelnut" that represents "all that is made." Julian is frequently depicted with a cat; though we can be fairly certain that Julian did not have a Siamese cat, this illustration by Sam West honors a beloved family pet.

First Sunday after Christmas

LI TIM-OI

Priest (1907–1992)

Arise, shine; for your light has come, and the glory of the Lord has risen upon you.

—*Isaiah 60:1*

✝ God is my strength, my song, and my salvation.

O God is the true God who is always with me.

⊕ I praise God unceasingly for His great mercy in allowing me to endure all tests.

• How true and sweet is the taste of God's mercy.

⊕ God's hand is always there to hold me up, to conquer the darkness and rampage.

• Whenever I am face to face with peril, His gracious hand holds me fast.

⊕ No one can take away the peace that comes from fulfilling God's will.

• God's grace is boundless. It is enough for me.

⊕ God delights in beautifying the world and everything in it.

• God wants us to have beautiful lives.

⊕ I will work hard for the Lord and do my best for the rest of my days in order to glorify Him and benefit His people.

O God's love and mercy are eternal.

✝ Faith surely triumphs over all. Hallelujah! God be praised.

O God, by the leading of a star you manifested your only Son to the peoples of the earth: Lead us, who know you now by faith, to your presence, where we may see your glory face to face; through Jesus Christ our Lord, who lives and reigns with you and the Holy Spirit, one God, now and for ever. *Amen.*

Florence Li Tim-Oi, the first woman ordained as a priest in the Anglican Communion, served the church with quiet strength and humble obedience throughout her life. Her courageous commitment to the Eucharist allowed Christians in war-torn Macao to receive the Bread of Life during the Japanese occupation in World War II.

Born in 1907 in the British colony of Hong Kong to Chinese Christian parents, Li was given the name of Tim-Oi, which means "much beloved daughter" by her father to signify his joy at having a girl child at a time when many families favored sons over daughters. He taught her the Lord's Prayer when she was a young child and hosted Bible study classes in the family living room. At her baptism she chose the name Florence because of her love of flowers and to honor Florence Nightingale, whose charitable service she admired deeply. In 1931, Tim-Oi attended the ordination of Deaconess Lucy Vincent, who challenged the women in attendance to follow in her footsteps and give their lives to the Chinese Church. "I am here. Please send me," Tim-Oi thought; three years later she enrolled at Union Theological College, Canton.

Following her graduation in 1938, the diocese sent Tim-Oi to a church in Hong Kong for two years, then to the nearby Portuguese territory of Macao. She was ordained to the diaconate on Ascension Day in 1941, and was soon performing worship services, baptisms, weddings, and funerals for the local

The Epiphany of the Lord

Anglican congregation. After Hong Kong was occupied by the Japanese, it became too dangerous for priests in China to travel across enemy lines into Macao, so in 1944, Bishop R. O. Hall, recognizing Li's priestly gifts, ordained her to the priesthood, making Li Tim-Oi not only the first woman priest in the Anglican Communion, but the first woman ordained as a priest in any church that claims to maintain apostolic succession. This action caused great controversy within the Anglican Communion, the leadership of which strongly disapproved of Li's ordination. When the war ended, at the request of the Chinese House of Bishops, Li Tim-Oi humbly and obediently agreed to surrender her license as a priest, but she did not give up her priestly orders, nor did she renounce her priestly vocation—she believed "the priesthood is a vocation for life. You have to be faithful to your vows to the end." She was then made the rector of the Anglican church in Hepu, near the Vietnamese border, where she provided pastoral services and helped to re-establish the Anglican church; although she did not celebrate the Eucharist, the parishioners referred to her as "priest," at Bishop Hall's instruction. Tim-Oi also helped to establish a maternity hospital in Hepu. Later, she joined the faculty of Union Theological College.

As part of the Chinese Communist Revolution, the government closed all churches in 1958; Li Tim-Oi was condemned as a counterrevolutionary. The Red Guards raided her home several times, destroyed much of her property and forced her to cut up her priestly vestments with scissors. She was then sent for "re-education" and forced to work on a farm for two years, where she was known as the "Captain of the Chickens." Her other labors included working in a factory, collecting firewood, and laboring in the taro fields. When the churches reopened in 1979, Tim-Oi resumed her public ministry.

After nearly three decades of "re-education," confinement, and forced labor, Li Tim-Oi received permission to leave China and join her family in Toronto in 1983. The Diocese of Montreal licensed her as a priest allowing her to joyfully resume her priestly duties, first in Montreal and later in Toronto. In 1991, she received an honorary doctorate of divinity from Trinity College, Toronto. Florence Li Tim-Oi died on February 26, 1992.

Florence Li Tim-Oi is commemorated by the Anglican Communion and the Lutheran Church on February 26, the date of her death; in the Episcopal Church she is commemorated on January 24, the anniversary of her ordination.

This prayer is taken from her memoir, *Raindrops of My Life*. In this illustration, I show her with the symbols of her priestly vocation and the elements of the Holy Eucharist hovering over her heart.

The Epiphany of the Lord

POLYCARP

Bishop of Smyrna and Martyr (ca. 69–156)

He commanded us to preach to the people and to testify that he is the one ordained by God as judge of the living and the dead.

—*Acts 10:42*

☩ Mercy unto you, and peace from God Almighty and from the Lord Jesus Christ, our Savior, be multiplied.

O I have greatly rejoiced with you in our Lord Jesus Christ because you follow the example of true love.

☩ Faith is followed by hope and preceded by love toward God, Christ, and our neighbor.

• Let us teach ourselves to walk in the commandments of the Lord.

☩ Pray for the enemies of the cross, that your fruit may be seen by all and that you may be perfect in Christ.

• Let us arm ourselves with the armor of righteousness.

☩ All things on heaven and earth are subject to God. Every spirit serves him.

• The will of God be done.

☩ "Eighty and six years have I served Him, and He never did me any injury: how then can I blaspheme my King and my Savior?"

• Hear me declare with boldness, "I am a Christian."

☩ Pray for all the saints. Pray also for those who govern, and for those who persecute you and hate you.

O I praise you, God, for all things, I bless you, I glorify you, along with the eternal heavenly high priest Jesus Christ, your beloved Son, through whom be glory to you, and with the Holy Spirit, now and for the ages to come.

☩ Keep yourself safe in the Lord Jesus Christ. Grace be with you all. *Amen.*

Father in heaven, who at the baptism of Jesus in the River Jordan proclaimed him your beloved Son and anointed him with the Holy Spirit: Grant that all who are baptized into his Name may keep the covenant they have made, and boldly confess him as Lord and Savior; who with you and the Holy Spirit lives and reigns, one God, in glory everlasting. *Amen.*

Polycarp, whose name means "much fruit," lived a life of great holiness; his faith in Jesus Christ was unshakable.

Polycarp was born around the year 69, shortly after the executions of Peter and Paul in Rome. Tradition holds that Polycarp was converted to Christianity by John the Evangelist and became his follower. According to Irenaeus, Polycarp could recite from memory the sayings and stories that he learned from the "eyewitnesses of the Word of Life"—people who had personally known Jesus. John appointed Polycarp to serve as bishop to the church in Smyrna, now Izmir, Turkey, an episcopate he held for nearly fifty years. He was widely regarded as an apostolic and prophetic teacher.

As bishop, Polycarp wrote a letter to the church at Philippi, exhorting them to stay strong in the faith. His letter shows us that the four Gospels and the epistles of Paul and John were treated as the Word of God by early Christians long before the biblical canon was established.

Polycarp was martyred at the age of eighty-six for failing to renounce Christ and swear an oath of allegiance to the Roman emperor. *The Martyrdom of Polycarp,* attributed to the early church fathers, is the first written account of a Christian martyrdom since Luke described the martyrdom of Stephen in the Acts of the Apostles.

When the Roman soldiers came to arrest Polycarp, he gave them food and drink, requesting only that they give him an hour to pray without disturbance before they led him away (in fact, he prayed for two hours and caused many solders to repent that they had come to arrest him). After praying, Polycarp announced, "The will of God be done," and he left peacefully with his captors.

Polycarp was brought before the Roman proconsul, who commanded him to renounce Christ and swear by Caesar instead. Polycarp refused, saying, "hear me declare it boldly, I am a Christian." He was then sentenced to be burned at the stake.

According to witnesses, after Polycarp was tied to a stake, he gave thanks to God that he should be considered worthy of martyrdom. After he finished his prayer, the fire was lit; the flames rose in a great arch, encircling Polycarp's body, but failing to consume it; witnesses claimed that the smoke had a fragrance like frankincense. When the fire failed to kill him, the executioner was commanded to stab Polycarp with a dagger. When Polycarp was stabbed, the witnesses said that a dove flew out of his body and that the blood from his wound put out the fire.

The feast day for Polycarp is celebrated throughout the Church on February 23.

The words of this prayer are taken from Polycarp's *Epistle to the Philippians* and from *The Martyrdom of Polycarp*. The illustration is adapted from a fifteenth-century woodcut depicting the martyrdom of Polycarp.

CHARBEL MAKLOUF

Priest, Monastic (1828–1898)

"'He on whom you see the Spirit descend and remain is the one who baptizes with the Holy Spirit.' And I myself have seen and have testified that this is the Son of God."

—John 1:33–34

✠ Keep silence in order to hear and understand the Lord's voice.

O Train yourselves for silence, a silence that listens, a silence that lives, a silence that is quite far from the calm of nothingness.

✠ Be monks in the midst of the world, even if you do not wear the habit.

• Every human being is a flame created by our Lord to enlighten the world.

✠ God illuminates the way for you, but it is up to you to walk in it.

• Live in the light of the truth that you grasp.

✠ Let Christ live in you, and you will live at the heart of the mystery of the universe, in the source of light.

• Carry the cross of Christ, and you will have the key to heaven.

✠ Let everyone fill his jar with the treasure of Christ, who is the only true treasure.

• Know where your treasure is and put your whole heart there.

✠ Be saints so as to sanctify the earth. If God's thoughts are in your minds and his love is in your hearts, his might will strengthen your arms and you will reach the goal.

O His Word is what guides you, and his Spirit is what fills your sails; thus you will arrive at the shore of light.

✠ Travel your path with the joy of the resurrection.

Second Sunday after the Epiphany

Almighty God, whose Son our Savior Jesus Christ is the light of the
world: Grant that your people, illumined by your Word and Sacraments,
may shine with the radiance of Christ's glory, that he may be known,
worshiped, and obeyed to the ends of the earth; through Jesus Christ
our Lord, who with you and the Holy Spirit lives and reigns, one God,
now and for ever. *Amen.*

*C*harbel (also spelled Sharbel) was born in a village in the high mountains
of Lebanon in 1828, to parents who were Maronite Christians. When
Charbel was three years old, his father, a mule driver, died while doing com-
pulsory service with the Turkish Army during its occupation of Lebanon. After
his mother remarried in 1833, Charbel lived in his parents' house, but under
his uncle's guardianship. He received a Christian education, learning to read
and write from the village priests. When he was a boy, the local villagers called
him "the saint," because he showed particular devotion to the Holy Eucharist
and carried his prayer book wherever he went.

His uncle, a priest, brought Charbel to the monastery of Our Lady of May-
fouq, where he began his novitiate with radiant joy. At the end of the one-year
novitiate, he entered the St. Maron Monastery in Annaya, Lebanon, where he
took the name of Charbel (which means "Story of God" in Syriac) to honor a
second-century martyr of the same name. In 1853, he made his vows of poverty,
obedience, and chastity, and became a monk of the Lebanese Maronite Order.
He was soon sent to study for the priesthood, and was ordained a priest in 1859.
He began the ascetic life of a monk at the monastery of St. Yaaqoub Al Hosson,
but was later called back to the St. Maron Monastery where he lived a life of
strict asceticism for sixteen years.

Second Sunday after the Epiphany

During his time at the monastery, miraculous events started to happen in Charbel's life. He drove off a poisonous snake and a swarm of locusts that had been endangering the local community by respectfully asking the pests to leave. Charbel spent so much time during the night praying and studying that the prior of the monastery grew concerned for his health and ordered that he not be given oil for his lamp. His fellow monks filled his lamp with water, instead, but when Charbel lit his lamp it burned steadily throughout the night. The prior, when informed of this phenomenon, determined that the hand of God was involved in the incident and Charbel was granted permission to withdraw from the world and live as a hermit, in 1875.

In his hermitage, he followed the strict rules of the Lebanese Maronite Order: eat only one meal a day, as sent by the monastery; abstain from meat and wine; sleep on the ground, no more than five hours per day, and observe strict silence. He lived in hermitage until his death twenty-three years later.

While celebrating Mass on December 18, 1898, Charbel suffered a stroke and fell to the ground, still holding the Host. For the next week he never regained full consciousness, but kept repeating "Father of truth, behold your Son," a line from the prayer he had been reciting when he was stricken, along with the names of Jesus, Mary, Joseph, plus the names Peter and Paul, the patron saints of his monastery. He died on Christmas Eve, and was buried at the monastery. According to witnesses, soon afterward the place of his burial was surrounded by a light of "extraordinary brightness" for forty-five days.

Four months after Charbel's death, the monks were given ecclesiastical permission to exhume his body, which was found to be incorrupt; his body was then placed in a special tomb which became a site of pilgrimage. In the first two years after his death, more than 1,200 miracles were reported to the monastery. His body was again exhumed in 1950 and exuded a "blood-like liquid" which the monks collected on linen cloths. Since his death, many miracles of healing have occurred in his name.

Saint Charbel is venerated on July 24 by the Roman Catholic Church and on the third Sunday in July in the Maronite Calendar.

Second Sunday after the Epiphany

This prayer is taken from the homilies that Charbel wrote during his time as a hermit. There are no known images of him that were made during his lifetime. On May 8, 1950, the hermit's birthday, four Maronite missionaries made a pilgrimage to his tomb. Father George Webby, a Maronite priest from Scranton, Pennsylvania, took a photo of the four standing by the wall of the monastery where Saint Charbel had lived. When the film was developed, an image of a monk with a white beard appeared next to the missionaries. The oldest monks, who had known Father Charbel, recognized the image immediately as the saint himself. Nearly all subsequent portraits of him have been based on Fr. Webby's 1950 photograph.

Second Sunday after the Epiphany

CHARLES DE FOUCAULD

Priest, Monastic (1858–1916)

The Lord is my light and my salvation; whom shall I fear? The Lord is the stronghold of my life; of whom shall I be afraid?

—*Psalms 27:1*

✠ My Lord and my God, come to my aid, so that I may do whatever you ask of me.

O I abandon myself to you, I entrust myself to you. Make of me what you will.

☩ Giving thanks for everything, I am ready for anything, I accept anything.

• Whatever you do with me, I will thank you for it.

☩ As long as your will is done in all your creatures, in all your children, in all those whom your heart loves,

• As long as your will is done in me, I desire nothing else.

☩ My Father, I put myself in your hands.

• My love requires me to give myself.

☩ I give my soul to you, Lord, with all the love in my heart.

• I put my soul in your hands, because I love you.

☩ I put myself in your hands with infinite trust, for you are my Father.

O I thank you for everything.

✠ My God, give me real faith! My God, I believe, help the little faith I have!

Give us grace, O Lord, to answer readily the call of our Savior Jesus Christ and proclaim to all people the Good News of his salvation, that we and the whole world may perceive the glory of his marvelous works; who lives and reigns with you and the Holy Spirit, one God, for ever and ever. *Amen.*

*C*harles de Foucauld, lived as a hermit among the Tuareg people of Algeria and Morocco. His contemplative vocation of prayer and adoration planted seeds that bore fruit after his death.

Brother Charles was born in Strasbourg in 1858, to a wealthy family of minor French nobility. After he was orphaned at age six, he lived with his devout grandfather, who hoped Charles would become a military officer. Although raised in the faith, his troubled adolescence left him doubting God's existence.

At eighteen, Charles enrolled in the prestigious Saint-Cyr military academy, seeking adventure. When his grandfather died, he inherited a small fortune which he spent on fine dining, expensive wines, gambling, and his mistress, Mimi. When his unit was sent to Algiers in 1880, Charles brought Mimi with him, disobeying a direct order. This resulted in suspension from the unit and his return to France. When fighting broke out in Algiers, Charles requested reinstatement and he was sent back to Algeria, this time leaving Mimi behind in France.

Against all odds, Charles proved to be an excellent soldier and leader in combat. The desert, he later wrote, had a purifying effect on his soul. After six months of pursuing Algerian rebels, his unit was posted back to barracks, whereupon Charles suffered a malaise of spirit. In 1882, he resigned from the army and began studying the history and cultures of North Africa, making plans to explore the Moroccan desert. He spent over two years on this quest, dressed as a peddler, so as not to draw the attention of robbers, and traveling with an adventurous Jewish rabbi as his guide. His published account of his desert adventures and explorations, accompanied by detailed maps and drawings, *Reconnaissance au Maroc,* was published in 1885, for which he was awarded a gold medal by the Geographical Society of Paris.

The piety of the Jews and Muslims he met during his desert explorations "produced in me a profound upheaval," Charles wrote, and "allowed me to glimpse something greater and more true than worldly occupations." He prayed, "My God, if you exist, let me come to know you." In 1886, when he was twenty-eight years old, he had a conversion experience after making confession to a local priest. After experiencing the living Christ, Charles said, "I could not do otherwise than live only for him."

Charles, eager to enter the monastic life, undertook a pilgrimage to the Holy Land to confirm his vocation. On his return in 1890, he took provisional vows and entered a Trappist monastery to live "a life in accordance with Christ's," first in France and later in Syria. At his abbot's request, Charles began studying for the priesthood, though he dreamed of starting a new, more ascetic monastic order. In 1897 his petition to become a hermit was granted; he left the monastery but renewed his vows of chastity and poverty, and remained under obedience to a spiritual director. He traveled to Nazareth where he became the chaplain for the Poor Clares, living in a shack outside the convent walls. It was here that he wrote his *Méditations* and began using the name of Brother Charles of Jesus.

Charles returned to France and was ordained a priest in 1901, a prerequisite for founding a new monastic order. Three months later he sailed to Algeria, where he served as chaplain to the French forces and as a witness to Christ among the desert tribes. Charles personified a "universal brotherhood," treating every guest to his desert hermitage as Christ. He learned the Tuareg language, made a four-volume Tuareg-French dictionary and compiled an anthology of Tuareg poetry. When asked how he spent his days, Brother Charles said, "I pray at night, work by day, love and contemplate Jesus unceasingly with my heart, in poverty, holiness, and love." Brother Charles was murdered by bandits in 1916 outside the door of his hermitage.

Charles de Foucauld is celebrated in the Anglican Communion and by the Roman Catholic Church on December 1.

This prayer is adapted from the *Méditations* and Prayer of Abandonment of Brother Charles de Foucauld. This drawing of him is based on a photograph taken at his hermitage; he is wearing the white habit of his Cistercian order, adorned with the emblem he adopted as his device *Jesus Caritas,* a cross atop a heart.

SERAPHIM OF SAROV

Monastic, Mystic (1754–1833)

Blessed are the peacemakers, for they will be called children of God.

—*Matthew 5:9*

✠ The true aim of our Christian life is to acquire the Holy Spirit of God.

O The Holy Spirit dwells mystically in the hearts of those who believe in our Lord God and Savior Jesus Christ.

♰ The grace of God's Holy Spirit appears in light inexpressible to all to whom God reveals its power.

• The grace of the Holy Spirit is my lamp and light.

♰ The more the heavenly riches of God's grace are given away, the more they increase in the giver.

• The Holy Spirit guides our steps into the way of peace.

♰ The Lord seeks a heart that is filled with love of God and neighbor.

• Only good deeds done for Christ's sake bring us the fruits of the Holy Spirit.

♰ In prayer we are granted to converse with our all-gracious and life-giving God and Savior.

• Great is the power of prayer; it brings the Spirit of God.

♰ When the mind and the heart are united in prayer, you feel that spiritual warmth which comes from Christ and fills the whole inner being with joy and peace.

O True enlightenment from the Lord is sent into the hearts of all who hunger and thirst for God's truth.

✠ The Spirit of God reminds us of the words of our Lord Jesus Christ, gladdening our hearts and guiding our steps into the way of peace.

Almighty and everlasting God, you govern all things both in heaven and on earth: Mercifully hear the supplications of your people, and in our time grant us your peace; through Jesus Christ our Lord, who lives and reigns with you and the Holy Spirit, one God, for ever and ever. *Amen.*

"Acquire a peaceful spirit, and thousands around you will be saved," said Saint Seraphim of Sarov, who regarded each person and each thing as a sacrament of the divine presence.

Saint Seraphim was born in Kursk, Russia, in 1754. When Seraphim was ten years old, he was stricken with a serious illness during which the Mother of God appeared to him and promised to heal him. Several days later, his condition miraculously improved after a procession bearing the *Theotokos* passed by his house. As a child, Seraphim avidly read Holy Scripture and the lives of the saints, especially the Desert Fathers and Mothers, who became a profound inspiration for him.

Seraphim sought vocational discernment during a pilgrimage to Kyiv, where a *staretz,* an Orthodox elder, foresaw that he would become a monk at the monastery at Sarov. After he returned home, he gave his share of his father's inheritance to his brother and left for Sarov, wearing a large brass pectoral cross given to him by his mother. He entered the monastery as a novitiate in 1778, at age twenty-four, and quickly impressed his superiors with his zeal and ascetic dedication. Seraphim "provisioned his soul" for his spiritual journey by standing before the icons and reading the Bible and patristics late into the night.

Four years after entering the monastery, Seraphim was struck by a grave illness that confined him to his bed for three years. When death seemed imminent, the monks held a prayer vigil for him, during which the Mother of God again visited Seraphim and his condition immediately improved. He made his monastic vows in 1786.

In 1793, Seraphim was ordained a priest and the following year he became the spiritual director of a small community of nuns in nearby Diveyevo. A year later, Seraphim left the company of his brothers for the solitude of the forest and took up residence in the monastery's hermitage, which he consecrated to the Virgin of Tenderness who had twice healed him from illness. At the hermitage, Seraphim spent his days singing hymns, reading Scripture, and constantly keeping the Name of Jesus on his lips. He returned to the monastery every Sunday to receive the Eucharist and to get bread and rations for the coming week, which he shared with the animals who lived near the hermitage.

Alone in his hut, Seraphim battled spiritual temptations and demons as well as anxiety and depression. To overcome his torments, he spent a thousand days and nights in prayer, kneeling on a granite rock, with frequent fasting. During this time, he survived by foraging for ground elder and other woodland plants, which he dried for use during the winter. One day, he was attacked by robbers who beat him and left him for dead. Seraphim was able to drag himself back to the monastery, where he convalesced for several months. When the robbers were caught and tried, the holy monk, who was left permanently hunched over from his injuries, interceded on their behalf. Upon returning to his hermitage, Seraphim entered a period of absolute silence, without returning weekly to the monastery for worship.

In 1810, the monastery's new abbot directed Seraphim to return. After fifteen years of silent devotion, Seraphim enclosed himself in a monastic cell which he only left at night, for walks. His brother monks brought food and the Blessed Sacrament directly to his cell. After five years, he received a sign during prayer to open his door and became a *staretz*, again providing spiritual direction for the nuns in Diveyevo, and many others—including, according to legend, Tsar Alexander I himself. He radiantly greeted pilgrims with the words, "My Joy, Christ is risen!" On New Year's Day in 1833, Father Seraphim gave the

Fourth Sunday after the Epiphany

monastery's icons a final kiss and went to his room to pray. The monks found him dead the next morning, kneeling before the Virgin of Tenderness.

The feast of Saint Seraphim of Sarov is celebrated by the Eastern Orthodox Church and in the Anglican Communion on January 2.

Although Saint Seraphim himself left no written record, many recorded the elder's words. The prayer is taken from *On Acquisition of the Holy Spirit* by Nicholas Motovilov. The illustration shows the saint praying to the Virgin of Tenderness at his hermitage, befriended by a local bear.

FREDERICK DOUGLASS

Prophetic Witness (1818–1895)

For the righteous will never be moved; they will be remembered forever.

—*Psalms 112:6*

☦ We, who have God and conscience on our side, have a majority against the universe.

⊙ It is not light that we need, but fire; it is not the gentle shower, but thunder. We need the storm, the whirlwind, and the earthquake.

☦ The whole history of the progress of human liberty shows that all concessions yet made to her august claims, have been born of earnest struggle.

• If there is no struggle, there is no progress.

☦ No man can put a chain about the ankle of his fellow man without at last finding the other end fastened about his own neck.

• In the struggle for justice, the only reward is the opportunity to be in the struggle.

☦ Power concedes nothing without a demand. It never has and it never will.

• I would unite with anybody to do right and with nobody to do wrong.

☦ Where justice is denied, where poverty is enforced, where ignorance prevails, and where any one class is made to feel that society is an organized conspiracy to oppress, rob, and degrade them, neither persons nor property will be safe.

• It is easier to build strong children than to repair broken men.

☦ God is most glorified when there is peace on earth and good will toward men.

⊙ A smile or a tear has no nationality; joy and sorrow speak alike to all nations, and they, above all the confusion of tongues, proclaim the brotherhood of man.

☦ Right is of no sex, Truth is of no color, God is the Father of us all, and we are all Brethren.

Set us free, O God, from the bondage of our sins, and give us the liberty of that abundant life which you have made known to us in your Son our Savior Jesus Christ; who lives and reigns with you, in the unity of the Holy Spirit, one God, now and for ever. *Amen.*

Frederic Augustus Washington Bailey was born around 1818 to an enslaved woman, but separated from her in his infancy. When he was eight, he was sent to a family in Baltimore, Maryland, where his enslaver's wife taught him the alphabet until her husband insisted that "knowledge unfits a child to be a slave." Overhearing this, Frederick understood that "knowledge was the pathway from slavery to freedom." He taught himself to read and write, often trading morsels of food to poor white children in exchange for instruction in reading. At fifteen, Frederick was sent back to rural Maryland where he endured many harsh beatings. He secretly organized a Sunday school where he taught more than forty enslaved people "to read the will of God."

His enslaver returned him to Baltimore where he fell in love with Anna Murray, a free Black woman. In 1838, Anna bought Frederick a train ticket to New York, which he used to escape slavery. Anna later joined him in New York and the couple were married. They moved to Massachusetts, adopted the surname "Douglass" and started a family. Frederick joined the African Methodist Episcopal Zion Church, becoming a licensed preacher. He was active in the abolitionist movement and quickly developed a reputation as a fiery orator, speaking throughout the Midwest, the Northeast, and the British Isles.

During his lifetime, he wrote three autobiographies, the first, *Narrative of the Life of Frederick Douglass, an American Slave,* published in 1845, was an instant success, selling more than 30,000 copies within five years. In this

Fifth Sunday after the Epiphany

account, Frederick decried the religious hypocrisy of many American Christians in scathing terms, pointing out that they were building churches with money raised from selling human beings, and that "he who proclaims it a religious duty to read the Bible, denies me the right of learning to read the name of the God who made me."

In his autobiography, Frederick commented, "I love the pure, peaceable, and impartial Christianity of Christ: I therefore hate the corrupt, slaveholding, women-whipping, cradle-plundering, partial and hypocritical Christianity of this land." In 1847, he began publishing an abolitionist newspaper, *The North Star,* a weekly paper with the motto "Right is of no sex, Truth is of no color, God is the Father of us all, and we are all Brethren." He continued writing and speaking out for the abolition of slavery and for women's rights. His most famous speech, "What to the Slave Is the Fourth of July?" was delivered in 1852, declaring that perpetuation of slavery "disregarded and trampled upon" the Bible, and he quoted the prophet Isaiah, calling out the sins of the people in the light of God's will for justice and freedom.

Frederick corresponded with many influential people, including Abraham Lincoln, John Brown, and Susan B. Anthony. In a letter to Harriet Beecher Stowe, he wrote, "our merciful Heavenly father, whose ear is ever open to the cries of the oppressed" favored the efforts of those who opposed slavery. His second autobiography, *My Bondage and My Freedom* was published in 1855.

During the Civil War, Frederick actively recruited Black soldiers for the Union army and met with President Lincoln to advocate for better pay and living conditions for Black soldiers. Following the Civil War, he moved to Washington, DC, and held numerous government appointments, including serving as a diplomat to Haiti. His third autobiography, *The Life and Times of Frederick Douglass,* was published in 1881.

From his early childhood, Frederick had a conviction that "slavery would not always be able to hold me in its foul embrace." This "living word of faith and spirit of hope departed not from me, but remained like ministering angels to cheer me through the gloom. This good spirit was from God, and to him

I offer thanksgiving and praise," he wrote. Douglass died in Washington, DC, in 1895.

Frederick Douglass is commemorated in the Anglican Communion on February 20.

This prayer is from the autobiographies and speeches of Frederick Douglass. This drawing is from a photograph taken around 1879, now in the National Archives and Records Administration.

GREGORY OF NYSSA

Bishop and Theologian (ca. 335–395)

With my whole heart I seek you; do not let me stray from your commandments. I treasure your word in my heart, so that I may not sin against you.

—*Psalms 119:10–11*

✠ The infinite beauty of God is constantly being discovered anew.

O The beauty that is reflected in all things should lead us to a yearning for that Beauty whose glory the heavens proclaim.

✠ You must wash away, by a life of virtue, the dirt that clings to your heart, then your divine beauty will once again shine forth.

• To stop on the path of virtue is to begin on the path of evil.

✠ The soul that pursues true virtue participates in God Himself, because God is infinite virtue.

• The path of those who rise to God is unlimited.

✠ Scripture leads our understanding upward to the higher levels of virtue.

• Make use of Scripture as your counselor.

✠ We shall be blessed with clear vision if we keep our eyes fixed on Christ, for he is our head, and in him there is no shadow of evil.

• No darkness can be seen by anyone surrounded by light.

✠ The man who avoids all bitterness will become beautiful because he has drawn near to Beauty; he will become luminous because he is in communion with the true light.

O We too, shall become luminous if we rise above this earthly darkness and draw near to the true Light which is Christ.

✠ As God continues to reveal Himself, we continue to wonder; and we never exhaust our desire to see more.

O God, the strength of all who put their trust in you: Mercifully accept our prayers; and because in our weakness we can do nothing good without you, give us the help of your grace, that in keeping your commandments we may please you both in will and deed; through Jesus Christ our Lord, who lives and reigns with you and the Holy Spirit, one God, for ever and ever. *Amen.*

The writings of Gregory of Nyssa lead us to a more profound understanding of mysteries of God. One of the most original thinkers of the early Church, his Bible commentaries shed new light on ancient texts.

Gregory was born between 330 and 335 in Cappadocia (central Turkey) to a devout and wealthy Christian family. His grandmother was a martyr and his parents, along with three siblings, all became saints. His parents both died while Gregory was young; it is likely that young Gregory was raised by his saintly siblings, Basil and Macrina.

Gregory received an excellent education in the Greek classics and liberal arts. As a young man, he was a follower of the Roman Emperor Julian, known as "the Apostate" for his humanist philosophy and rejection of Christianity. Later he became a professor of rhetoric.

The biography of Gregory of Nyssa is closely linked to that of his older brother, Basil the Great and their close friend Gregory Nazianzus. The three of them, collectively known as the Cappadocian Fathers, greatly influenced the doctrine of the Holy Trinity. They were the theological architects of the victory of the Orthodox faith over Arianism in the fourth century; all three are recognized as saints, in both the Eastern and Western Church.

Sixth Sunday after the Epiphany

Basil traveled throughout Egypt and Palestine, learning the ways of the Desert Fathers. When he returned to Cappadocia in 358, he settled into a monastic life at the family estate in Pontus, across the Iris river from the religious community that his sister Macrina had established.

It seems that Gregory of Nyssa's conversion back to the Christian faith was strongly influenced by the example of his sister Macrina and the words of Gregory of Nazianzus. The younger Gregory was ordained a priest sometime before 372, when his brother Basil, who was now the bishop of Caesarea, appointed him bishop of Nyssa. At that time, the Arians were at the height of their influence, and Basil wished to surround himself with bishops he could trust.

Gregory's Arian rivals accused the newly appointed bishop of mishandling church funds and irregularities concerning his appointment by his brother Basil. Illness prevented Gregory from appearing to defend himself against these charges, so he was deposed in 376 and banished from Nyssa by the anti-Nicene Emperor Valens. When Valens was killed in battle against the Goths, two years later, Gregory was restored to his bishopric, much to the acclaim of the local residents.

After his brother Basil's death in 379, Gregory became a prolific writer, completing many of Basil's unfinished theological works. Shortly after Basil's death, Gregory wrote *On the Soul and Resurrection,* based on the life and sayings of his sister Macrina, whom he called "the Teacher." Working with Gregory of Nazianzus, the two were the principal theological architects of the victory of Nicene orthodoxy over the various forms and degrees of Arianism at the "ecumenical" Council of Constantinople in 381. For the next five years, Gregory of Nyssa played a prominent role in the leadership of the Church in Asia Minor, through his theological writings and his efforts to restore ecclesiastical unity.

After around 385, Gregory seemed to have stepped back from his ecclesiastical responsibilities to devote his full energy to writing. Although the exact date of his death is unknown; he disappears from records after 394. Gregory of Nyssa is remembered as a champion of Orthodoxy and an important contributor to Christian mystical spirituality.

Sixth Sunday after the Epiphany

The feast day for Gregory of Nyssa in the Eastern Church, the Roman Catholic Church, and the Lutheran Church is January 10. In the Anglican Communion he is commemorated on March 9 or on July 19.

This prayer is taken from his sermons, *The Life of Moses,* and his *Commentary on the Song of Songs.* This image is drawn after a fourteenth-century icon of Gregory written by Theophanes the Greek.

TOYOHIKO KAGAWA

Social Reformer (1888–1960)

Give to everyone who begs from you, and do not refuse anyone who wants to borrow from you. You have heard that it was said, "You shall love your neighbor and hate your enemy." But I say to you, "Love your enemies and pray for those who persecute you."

—*Matthew 5:42–44*

☦ Father God: we confess with shame that we are always choosing things that are selfish, comfortable, too much according to our own preferences and tastes.

○ Give us strength to purify our country and our society from the spirit of selfishly seeking the interests of people who are like ourselves.

☦ Only by service to others can a man, or nation, be godlike.

• Only by living in simplicity can we learn the beauty of God.

☦ The love of Christ is not a religion of fear. It is the fountain of love and joy and life.

• We must live forever in the love of Christ.

☦ The mystical experience of the Holy Spirit is the intuitive recognition of the love of God.

• The Holy Spirit and love cannot be separated.

☦ When we come into the consciousness of the Holy Spirit, even though there are hardships, they are nothing.

• We must weave the Holy Spirit into our daily living.

☦ When we have the will of Christ, there is an outflow of prayer. Our love widens until it includes not only all humanity, but all created things as well.

○ The words "in my name" mean having a heart that would try to love the universe with the feeling of God.

☦ Grant that we may hold fast in unswerving determination to our resolution to follow the Way of the Cross.

O Lord, you have taught us that without love whatever we do is worth nothing; Send your Holy Spirit and pour into our hearts your greatest gift, which is love, the true bond of peace and of all virtue, without which whoever lives is accounted dead before you. Grant this for the sake of your only Son Jesus Christ, who lives and reigns with you and the Holy Spirit, one God, now and for ever. *Amen.*

Toyohiko Kagawa brought the redeeming love of Christ to those living in abject poverty, transforming prayer and compassion into social action.

Toyohiko was born in Kobe, Japan, in 1888, the child of a samurai and his geisha. When his father and mother both died four years later, young Toyohiko went to live with his father's wife. He excelled in primary school, despite his unhappy home life. Toyohiko then went to live with an older brother in the city of Tokushima, where he attended middle school. When he was fifteen, Toyohiko began learning English from Presbyterian missionaries who taught him about a father in heaven who loved him unconditionally. Gradually, the lessons of the missionaries inspired Toyohiko to be baptized into the Christian faith.

Toyohiko decided to enter seminary, and soon began preaching in the slums of Kobe. While in seminary, he contracted tubercular pneumonia and was hospitalized for four months, after which he went to convalesce by himself in a remote fishing village. Though his strength gradually returned, the illness was not entirely cured, and would recur intermittently throughout his life.

When Toyohiko resumed his studies, he lived in a two-room shack in the slums which he shared with others who needed housing; he often preached to the poor in the streets. He also started a Sunday school and soon was teaching a class for more than seventy children, who referred to him as *Sensei*. His evenings were spent teaching the adults and working with longshoremen to help them organize for better working conditions.

In 1913 Toyohiko married Haru, a factory worker who had come to hear him preach. The following year, he came to America and enrolled in Princeton Theological Seminary, while Haru stayed in Japan to continue his work for social reform. After receiving his Bachelor of Divinity degree from Princeton in 1917, he returned to Japan, where he worked for better salaries and labor conditions for the working poor, advocating a response to poverty based on the teachings from the Sermon on the Mount. He was arrested twice for his advocacy work and wrote two more books in prison, including one describing his experiences in the Kobe slums.

In 1924 he made his first speaking tour of Europe and the United States, bringing a message of pacifism and anti-imperialism. He earned the disfavor of his government in the 1930s and 1940s for apologizing to the Chinese people for Japan's aggression against them, earning him yet another arrest. In the early 1940s, he decried Japan's military buildup and traveled to the United States to promote greater understanding and friendship between the two nations.

During World War II, Toyohiko remained in Japan and opposed the war. After the war, the Japanese prime minister appointed him as an advisor to the cabinet, giving him a seat in the nation's House of Peers. In 1946 *Time* magazine named him "Japan's number one Christian." During speaking tours, Kagawa called on his audiences to apply the spirit of Christ to save the world in the Atomic Age; he spoke of ending world hunger as a prerequisite for world peace.

Toyohiko was a prolific writer, authoring more than 100 books on topics as varied as economics, Christian living, and poetry; he donated the proceeds from the sale of these books to help the poor. He was nominated for the Nobel Prize for both literature and peace. He died in Tokyo in 1960. His last words were, "Please do your best for world peace and the church in Japan."

Kagawa Toyohiko is commemorated on April 23 in the Anglican Communion and in the Lutheran Church.

Seventh Sunday after the Epiphany

This prayer is taken from his book, *Meditations on the Cross*. This illustration was inspired by a portrait of Toyohiko Kagawa by Jason Landsel for the August 2022 issue of *Plough* magazine, based on a photograph of Toyohiko taken when he was on a speaking tour of the United States in the 1940s. The original photograph is owned by the Burke Library Archives of the Union Theological Seminary in New York, New York.

Seventh Sunday after the Epiphany

PERPETUA AND FELICITY

Martyrs (born ca. 180–202)

He alone is my rock and my salvation, my fortress; I shall not be shaken. On God rests my deliverance and my honor; my mighty rock, my refuge is in God.

—*Psalms 62:6–7*

☩ Come first, enter and greet your Lord.

○ It is my privilege to converse with the Lord, whose kindness is so great.

　✢ "Father, can this little pitcher lying here be called by any other name than what it is?" Her father said, "No."

　• Neither can I call myself anything other than what I am, a Christian.

　✢ The day of their victory shone forth, and they proceeded from the prison into the amphitheater, joyous and of brilliant countenances.

• We are not placed in our own power, but in the power of God.

✢ When the populace called for them, they first kissed one another, that they might consummate their martyrdom with the kiss of peace.

• It will happen as God wills, for we are all in his power.

✢ We had suffered and we were gone forth from the flesh, beginning to be borne by four angels into the east, looking upwards, as if ascending a gentle slope. And being set free, we saw the boundless light.

• This is what the Lord promised to us; we have received the promise.

✢ You must all stand fast in the faith, and love one another, do not be weakened by what we have gone through.

○ Thanks be to God, that joyous as I was in the flesh, I am now more joyous here.

☩ Farewell, and be mindful of my faith; and let not these things disturb, but confirm you.

Most loving Father, whose will it is for us to give thanks for all things, to fear nothing but the loss of you, and to cast all our care on you who care for us: Preserve us from faithless fears and worldly anxieties, that no clouds of this mortal life may hide from us the light of that love which is immortal, and which you have manifested to us in your Son Jesus Christ our Lord; who lives and reigns with you, in the unity of the Holy Spirit, one God, now and for ever. *Amen.*

The steadfast faith of Perpetua, Felicity, and their companions inspires all Christians to remain firm during times of great trial.

Vibia Perpetua, a well-educated noblewoman, was born in the North African city of Carthage (now Tunis) around the year 180. The daughter of a Christian mother and pagan father, she had recently given birth to a son when she was arrested and imprisoned. Felicity, a pregnant enslaved woman, and three other catechumens were also arrested; a sixth voluntarily joined the group in solidarity. Perpetua kept a diary of her experiences during their imprisonment; it is the first diary of a Christian woman that has been preserved.

The five catechumens were baptized shortly after their arrest; a few days later they were condemned to be thrown to the wild beasts and held in a dungeon. Perpetua vividly describes her terror in being lodged "in such a dark hole," her yearning for her infant son and the stifling heat in the crowded prison cells. Perpetua was granted permission for her baby to stay with her, so she could nurse him while she was in prison. With her son at her breast, Perpetua says her prison was transformed into a palace, and she endured the rest of her confinement joyfully.

Felicity was an enslaved woman from another household who was eight months pregnant when she was arrested. Under Roman law, the execution of a pregnant woman was prohibited, as the unborn child was considered the property of the enslaver. As the scheduled execution drew near, Felicity was distraught that she might not be allowed to die with her companions, and would be left to die alone. Her fellow prisoners were also saddened, as they "were afraid that they would have to leave behind so fine a companion to travel alone on the same road of hope."

The small group of Christian prisoners "poured out abundant prayer to God" that Felicity would deliver her baby early. Miraculously, immediately after their prayer Felicity went into labor, giving birth to a daughter after a difficult and painful delivery. During her labor, she was taunted in her pain by a prison guard, to which Felicity replied, "What I am suffering now, I suffer by myself, but at the time" of my martyrdom, "another will be inside me who will suffer for me, just as I shall be suffering for him." Felicity's early delivery was seen as a sign from God that the Holy Spirit would be present with the group throughout the ordeals of their martyrdom. Felicity's daughter was later adopted by a member of the local Christian community.

The night before her death, Perpetua gave her diary to another Christian, who added an eyewitness account of the martyrs' deaths. The group was to be killed as part of the birthday celebration for the son of Roman Emperor Septimius Severus. On the day of their martyrdom (which they called "the day of our victory"), the prisoners were brought to the arena to face the wild beasts. A leopard, a bear, and a wild boar had been selected for the three men (one had died during their imprisonment), and a "mad heifer" was selected for the women, matching the gender of the beast to that of the women.

Perpetua and Felicity were scourged by gladiators, stripped naked, wrapped in rope nets, and placed in an arena with a wild cow to be tossed and gored. Even the bloodthirsty crowd was horrified to see the young women treated in this way, so the women were clad in tunics and returned to the arena. After they had survived being ravaged by the wild beast, a gladiator was ordered to kill them with his sword. Perpetua and Felicity "got up and went to the [execution] spot on their own accord, and kissing one another they sealed their martyrdom with the ritual kiss of peace." The gladiator struck bone on his first attempt, so Perpetua put the point of his spear on her own neck, facing her martyrdom with courage and grace.

Perpetua and Felicity are honored on February 1 in the Eastern Orthodox Church and on March 7 in the Western Church.

This prayer is taken from *The Passion of Perpetua and Felicity,* and intersperses Perpetua's own words with the narrative account of the martyrdom. This illustration was inspired by a beautiful icon by the master iconographer Brother Robert Lentz, OFM.

DIETRICH BONHOEFFER

Pastor and Theologian (1906–1945)

More than that, I regard everything as loss because of the surpassing value of knowing Jesus Christ my Lord. For his sake, I have suffered the loss of all things, and I regard them as rubbish, in order that I may gain Christ . . .

—*Phil. 3:8*

✠ God, I call to you early in the morning, help me to pray and collect my thoughts; I cannot do so alone.

O You abide with me when all men fail me. It is Your will that I should know You and turn to You.

⸸ My Creator and my Savior, this day belongs to you. My time is in your hands.

• Lord, whatever this day may bring—your name be praised.

⸸ Father in heaven, praise and thanks be to you for all your goodness and faithfulness in my life thus far.

• I trust your grace and commit myself entirely into your hand.

⸸ Lord Jesus Christ, you do not forget me and you seek me.

• Lord, I hear your call and follow. Help me!

⸸ Holy Spirit, grant me the love for God and others that purges all hate and bitterness.

• Teach me to discern Jesus Christ and to do his will.

⸸ Whoever I am, Thou knowest, O God, I am Thine!

O I am with you and you are with me, my God. Lord, I await your salvation and your kingdom.

✠ Let me sleep in peace beneath your protection and preserve me from the assaults of darkness. I commend to you my body and soul. God, your holy name be praised. *Amen.*

O God, who before the passion of your only begotten Son revealed his glory upon the holy mountain: Grant to us that we, beholding by faith the light of his countenance, may be strengthened to bear our cross, and be changed into his likeness from glory to glory; through Jesus Christ our Lord, who lives and reigns with you and the Holy Spirit, one God, for ever and ever. *Amen.*

"When Christ calls a man, he bids him come and die." These were the prophetic words of Dietrich Bonhoeffer who answered the Lord's call, even unto death. Dietrich Bonhoeffer was unafraid to speak the truth in times of social, political, and theological crisis, finding his freedom in serving God.

Born in 1906, Dietrich Bonhoeffer grew up in a wealthy, secular German household on the outskirts of Berlin, where his father was a professor of psychiatry and neurology. When he was thirteen, a year after his brother Walter was killed in World War I, Dietrich declared that he wanted to become a theologian and to reform a church that his family saw as irrelevant.

Dietrich studied theology at the universities of Tübingen and Berlin, where he was strongly influenced by Karl Barth's "theology of revelation." He received his Doctor of Theology degree from Berlin University, *summa cum laude,* at age twenty-one, after which, in 1928–29, he went to Barcelona, Spain, to serve as an assistant pastor. In 1930, Bonhoeffer went to New York to attend Union Theological Seminary for postdoctoral studies. There, he attended services of the Abyssinian Baptist Church in Harlem, where the passion of the preaching and singing awakened him to the need for the Church to speak for the oppressed.

After his return to Germany, Bonhoeffer was ordained in the Old-Prussian United church in 1931 and became a lecturer in theology at the University of

Berlin. He was an early opponent of Nazism and their antisemitism, delivering a radio address that attacked the cult of the Führer two days after Hitler's installation as Chancellor in 1933. From September 1933 to April 1935, Bonhoeffer served as pastor to several German-speaking congregations in London, leading them to disavow the German Evangelical Church, which had aligned with the Nazi party.

When he returned to Germany in 1935, he became a leading spokesman for the Confessing Church, the heart of the German Church's movement to resist the Nazis, and was a founder of Finkenwalde, a biblical-based church community that served as the underground seminary of the Confessing Church. The Gestapo closed Finkenwalde in 1937 and the following year banned Bonhoeffer from Berlin; however, the seminary continued covert religious training until 1940. During this time, Dietrich wrote *The Cost of Discipleship* (1937) and *Life Together* (1938), as well as studies on the Sermon on the Mount and the Pauline epistles.

In 1939, Dietrich returned to Union Theological Seminary to work with Reinhold Niebuhr but returned to Germany after only a few weeks, feeling drawn to be present with the German Church in its "time of trial." Once home, he decried the Church's silence, saying that it was "guilty of the deaths of the weakest and most defenseless brothers of Jesus Christ."

Bonhoeffer eventually joined the German Resistance and served as a double agent within the German military intelligence service where he helped Jews escape to Switzerland. When this was discovered, he was arrested by the Gestapo at his parents' home in April 1943. He was jailed for eighteen months at Tegel Prison, a military facility near Berlin, where he was allowed to read, write, and receive occasional visitors. However, when his name was discovered in the papers of a leader of the plot to assassinate Hitler, he was then moved from Tegel, ending up at the Buchenwald concentration camp.

Two months later, he was transferred to Flossenbürg, where he was convicted and executed by hanging, along with six other "conspirators" one month before Germany's surrender to the Allied forces. Though many regard him as one of the most important theologians of the twentieth century, Archbishop Desmond

Tutu said his greatest legacy is that he "maintained his faith in God even in the midst of incredible darkness." This prayer is taken from his *Letters and Papers from Prison,* published posthumously.

> Dietrich Bonhoeffer is commemorated on April 9 in the Lutheran Church and the Anglican Communion; the Anglican Church of Canada commemorates him and Maximilian Kolbe together on August 14. This image depicts him wearing the triangular badge worn by political prisoners.

Last Sunday after the Epiphany

ANTHONY OF EGYPT

Monastic (251–356)

Then Jesus was led up by the Spirit into the wilderness to be tempted by the devil.

—*Matthew 4:1*

✠ We are servants of the Lord and we owe a service to Him who created us.

O If we help our brother, we have helped God, but if we scorn our brother, we have sinned against Christ.

✟ Our life and our death are with our neighbor.

• Seek after that which will lead you to heaven.

✟ A good creator must necessarily have made the soul good.

• We should protect our soul with unceasing vigilance.

✟ The Lord has entrusted our soul to us: let us keep it in the same state as we received it.

• Protect yourselves with the sign of the cross.

✟ A pure life and fearless faith in God are powerful weapons against the demons.

• The virtue that is within us only requires the human will.

✟ Without temptation, no one can be saved.

O Whatever you do, do it according to the testimony of Holy Scripture.

✠ Wherever you may be, have God always before your eyes.

Almighty God, whose blessed Son was led by the Spirit to be tempted by Satan: Come quickly to help us who are assaulted by many temptations; and, as you know the weaknesses of each of us, let each one find you mighty to save; through Jesus Christ your Son, our Lord, who lives and reigns with you and the Holy Spirit, one God, now and for ever. *Amen.*

Saint Anthony has been called a "holy hero" for his wisdom, spiritual strength, and profound humility. Most of what we know about his life comes from *Vita S. Antoni* by Saint Athanasius, who knew him personally.

Anthony was born Upper Egypt in 251, the son of "well-born and devout parents." His parents died when he was about eighteen years old, leaving him with a sizable inheritance and the care of his younger sister. A short time later, Anthony heard the Gospel passage in which Jesus tells the rich young man to sell his possessions and give the money to the poor, in order to have treasure in heaven (Matt. 19:21). So Anthony sold his parents' estate, and, after setting aside money for the care of his sister, whom he entrusted to "faithful virgins of good repute," he gave the rest of his money to the poor and began a life of solitude.

Anthony moved to a small dwelling not far from his village and began living a life of rigorous austerity. He sought out holy men, absorbing from each one their "various individual gifts," striving to imitate their virtues. It was at this time that Anthony first entered spiritual warfare with the devil, resisting his temptations by constant prayer and singing. Eventually, he moved to some old tombs, where a friend brought him food and water. There the devil continued his assault on Anthony, but his spiritual resolve grew even stronger.

At the age of about thirty-five, Anthony sought greater solitude and withdrew even further into the desert, adopting a yet more rigorous Rule of Life. There, he came upon a deserted fort, full of venomous snakes which fled when Anthony took up residence. He blocked the entrance to the fort with stones and lived alone for the next twenty years. Twice a year, a monk would bring a six-month supply of bread which he would toss over a wall to Anthony. Demons continued to torment the holy hermit, but the Lord's power continued to grow in him.

Finally, in 306, after twenty years alone in the desert, Anthony ended his solitude to address a group of monks who had gathered, hoping to receive instruction from the blessed hermit. Instead of being a grizzled old hermit, Anthony emerged from his fort with a beautiful countenance, surrounded by an aura of holiness. Anthony guided the many monks who had gathered around him with fatherly affection. His remarks to the monks are considered to be the first monastic Rule for communal living.

In 311, Anthony was called to Alexandria to help support Christians imprisoned and sentenced to martyrdom. When he returned to the desert a year or two later, he founded a second monastery on the east bank of the Nile, then he retreated to a remote mountaintop, where he lived with his disciple Macarius. In 338, summoned by the bishop of Alexandria, he helped refute the Arian heresy. After this, he lived the remainder of his life in solitude. He died in 356 at the age of 105 and was interred in a grave next to his cell.

Saint Anthony is celebrated throughout the Church on January 17.

This prayer comes from the advice Saint Anthony gave to the assembled monks after he emerged from twenty years of solitude. The temptation of Saint Anthony in the desert has been portrayed by many of the greatest artists in the history of Western art. This illustration is inspired by a painting by Salvador Dalí that shows the great saint kneeling naked in the desert. In the original painting, Anthony takes up a small space in the lower left corner of the canvas, confronting demons that tower over him, representing lust, wealth, and the comforts of secular life. He is protected, as we all are, only by the Cross of Christ.

First Sunday in Lent

MARGARET OF CORTONA

Monastic (1247–1297)

The Lord will keep you from all evil; he will keep your life. The Lord will keep your going out and your coming in from this time on and forevermore.

—Psalms 121:7–8

✞ My Lord King, glory of the saints, great Jesus, you are my eternal God!

O My soul is greater than the world since it possesses you, you whom heaven and earth do not contain.

✞ Lord, I have tasted of you and my soul has felt the glory of paradise.

• My heart and body are exalted in the living God.

✞ I will not fear any creature nor any temptation because of the hope which I have placed in God, calling me back to his grace.

• The Almighty will comfort my soul.

✞ O sweet name above all others that has the power to call me to grace and redeem me by his blood!

• Lord Jesus, I seek you alone. Look kindly on my faith.

✞ Through your infinite mercy, Lord, I beg you to make my heart and my life conform perfectly to your love.

• Lord, you are my life, I live only for you.

✞ I ask you for perfect knowledge of your goodness and a perfect loving heart.

O O compassionate Lord, for the love of the Blessed Virgin and all your saints, forgive all who have offended me in whatever way, and for whatever reason. I implore you generously to give them eternal joys. Please pardon them.

✞ My Lord, bless all who are in the garden of your love.

O God, whose glory it is always to have mercy: Be gracious to all who have gone astray from your ways, and bring them again with penitent hearts and steadfast faith to embrace and hold fast the unchangeable truth of your Word, Jesus Christ your Son; who with you and the Holy Spirit lives and reigns, one God, for ever and ever. *Amen.*

After a troubled and turbulent youth, Margaret of Cortona underwent a total conversion of the heart, showing us the dramatic power of repentance and redemption.

Margaret was born to a family of farmers in the Tuscan village of Laviano in 1247. Her mother, a pious woman who taught Margaret the basics of the Christian faith, died when Margaret was about seven. Soon thereafter, her father remarried a woman who treated Margaret and her siblings very harshly, leading her to run away from home as a young teenager. Margaret, a young woman of exceptional beauty, took up residence with a young nobleman named Arsenio, with whom she later had a son, though the couple were never married. She enjoyed the opulence and luxury of life in his castle, despite the disapproval of Arsenio's parents.

When Margaret was in her early twenties, Arsenio left the castle one day, but only his dog returned. She followed the dog into the forest and discovered Arsenio's body partially buried under an oak tree, murdered by robbers. Perceiving this to be God's judgment on her lifestyle, Margaret repented, gave away her possessions, and returned to her father's house, but, at the urging of her stepmother, he banished her from their house.

She and her son then went to Cortona in about 1273, where they found accommodations with a local noblewoman. Margaret surrendered herself in obedience to the local Franciscans, who were known for their kindness to sinners and beggars; her confession lasted eight days. She resolved to spend the rest of her life in prayer and penance for her past lifestyle, moving into a small cottage among the poor and living off alms.

In Cortona, Margaret came under the spiritual direction of Fra Giunta Benegnati and petitioned the Franciscans to be admitted into their lay order. After three years, Margaret had so impressed the friars with her humility, piety, and change of heart that she was admitted to the Third Order of Saint Francis. Margaret embraced her new vows and offered herself completely to the Lord through service to the poor and penitential practices of prolonged fasting, sleeping on the bare earth, and other bodily mortifications; her son went to live and study at the Franciscan friary in nearby Arezzo.

Margaret became known in Cortona for her generosity, sharing with the city's poor whatever food she had. In fervent devotion, she often recited hundreds of Our Fathers and Hail Marys daily; many were converted by her devout example. In 1286, the bishop of Arezzo granted Margaret a charter to establish a hospital for the poor, which she ran with the help of other Franciscan tertiaries.

It was at this time Margaret began to receive ecstatic visions of Christ and to converse with him through mystical communion. In these visions, Christ urged her to "love all creatures, neither judging nor condemning anyone." She was widely recognized for her holiness, attracting pilgrims from throughout Italy, France, and Spain for her advice and blessing.

In 1288, Margaret received permission to withdraw from her cell at the convent and move to a solitary hermitage at the edge of the city to devote herself entirely to prayer and contemplation. Her first year of solitary life was one of spiritual desolation, in which she struggled with temptations and other assaults of Satan that left her feeling abandoned by God. But Margaret persisted in praising God and after this dark night passed, she was graced with eight years of loving contemplation and communion with her Lord. Margaret of Cortona died at the age of fifty on February 22, 1297. Many miracles, including restoration of sight, hearing, and speech, as well as the cure of physical, mental, and spiritual ailments were reported at the site of her grave.

Second Sunday in Lent

The feast day for Margaret of Cortona in the Roman Catholic Church is May 16; she is commemorated in the Anglican Communion on February 22.

This prayer is taken from Margaret's visions, as recorded by her confessor Fra Giunta Benegnati, who wrote her first *vita*. The illustration is based on a painting by Giovanni Battista Piazzetta (1683–1754).

PADRE PIO

Priest and Mystic (1887–1968)

Suffering produces endurance, and endurance produces character, and character produces hope, and hope does not disappoint us, because God's love has been poured into our hearts through the Holy Spirit that has been given to us.

—Romans 5:3–5

☩ Loving Father, touch me now with your healing hands, for I believe that your will is for me to be well in mind, body, soul, and spirit.

O If we are imitators of Jesus Christ as we undergo the battles of life, we too will participate in His victories.

☩ The bitterness of our trial will be sweetened by the heavenly Father with the balm of his goodness and mercy.

• Lord, I trust in your power and grace that sustain and restore me.

☩ Protect me from the cunning of the adversary, and lift me up when I am being tempted.

• Stay beside me at all times; never stop watching over me.

☩ A soul in the fire of tribulation will become refined gold, worthy to shine in the kingdom of heaven.

• Let the fire of your healing love pass through my entire body.

☩ My heart is invaded by a fire of living love, a delicate, sweet flame that consumes but causes no pain.

• God is present wherever there is a desire for his love.

☩ Entrust yourself to God, thank him for everything, and you will defy and conquer all the wrath of hell.

O Let us always trust in divine mercy, and we will increasingly experience how good the Lord is.

☩ Father, fill me with your Holy Spirit, empower me to do your works that my life will bring glory and honor to your holy name.

Third Sunday in Lent

Almighty God, you know that we have no power in ourselves to help ourselves: Keep us both outwardly in our bodies and inwardly in our souls, that we may be defended from all adversities which may happen to the body, and from all evil thoughts which may assault and hurt the soul; through Jesus Christ our Lord, who lives and reigns with you and the Holy Spirit, one God, for ever and ever. *Amen.*

Padre Pio lived a life of profound physical and spiritual suffering, yet is remembered for his joyful life and deep faith.

Padre Pio was born to a devout farming family in Pietrelcina, Italy, in 1887. He consecrated himself to Jesus at the age of five, and began taking on penances to demonstrate his devotion to God. From his earliest memory, he had conversations with Jesus, Mary, and his guardian angel.

Pio was an eager student, though he received only three years of formal schooling. When he was ten, he met a Capuchin and declared to his parents, "I want to be a friar with a beard!" Told that he would need additional schooling to become a priest, his father left for America in 1899 to earn the money for Pio's tuition.

In January 1903, Pio received visions that confirmed his vocation and revealed that his life in religion would be a continual struggle against the forces of evil. Two weeks later, Pio became a novitiate in the Capuchin order, receiving his tonsure and habit. After a yearlong novitiate, he took his temporary vows and began his studies for the priesthood. The following year, he was ordained a deacon and took his solemn vows; in 1910 he was ordained a priest.

After his ordination, Padre Pio experienced numerous physical and spiritual trials, including prolonged attacks of vomiting, violent coughing, severe headaches, and high fevers; he also experienced spiritual torment by demons.

Third Sunday in Lent

His persistent illness required him to live away from his religious community between 1911 and 1916, yet Pio remained true to his vocation. In 1916 Pio was ordered to the friary at San Giovanni Rotondo, where he would remain until his death in 1968. There, he provided spiritual direction to many, celebrated the Holy Eucharist with great devotion, and took confessions.

During his lifetime, Pio received numerous spiritual graces and experienced mystical phenomena that have led him to be called the twentieth century's greatest thaumaturge, or wonder worker. In addition to his visions and locutions, Pio had the gifts of healing, prophesy, tongues, and reading souls; he also experienced bilocation, levitation, and transverberation, and received the stigmata.

As his extraordinary gifts became known to the public, pilgrims flocked to the friary to make their confession to him and attend the masses he celebrated; his vestments had to be locked away from souvenir hunters who would snip off pieces of his robes. Some priests, especially those who feared that he was drawing parishioners—and their contributions—away from their churches, doubted the authenticity of his gifts and spread rumors of financial impropriety. His archbishop, who had a personal vendetta against Pio, suggested that the miracles, including the stigmata, were a fraud and that a cult was forming around him; he was also accused of sexual impropriety.

These allegations resulted in two investigations by the Vatican. In an attempt to quell his growing popularity, the Holy Office ordered Pio to refrain from celebrating Mass in public and forbade him from answering letters during 1921 and 1922, though these privileges were later restored. In 1931, after a second investigation, Pio was suspended from all public ministry, though these restrictions also were later eased. Finally, in 1964, Pope Paul VI ordered that Padre Pio be allowed to "exercise his ministry in full liberty."

Beginning in the 1960s, Padre Pio's frail health began to further deteriorate and his stigmata began to heal. The fiftieth anniversary of Padre Pio's visible stigmatization was commemorated on September 22, 1968, with Pio, then very frail, celebrating High Mass. He died peacefully the following morning with his rosary in his hands; his last words were, "Jesus . . . Mary."

Third Sunday in Lent

The feast day for Padre Pio is celebrated on September 23 by the Roman Catholic Church.

This prayer was taken from the letters of Padre Pio. The image was inspired by the graphic art of Chandran Crasta.

SOR JUANA INÉS DE LA CRUZ

Monastic, Poet, Theologian (ca. 1648–1695)

Live as children of light—for the fruit of the light is found in all that is good and right and true. Try to find out what is pleasing to the Lord. Take no part in the unfruitful works of darkness, but instead expose them.

—*Eph. 5:8–9*

✠ O mystery of the Incarnation! O Incarnation of the Word! O union most happy for us: that of God and humankind!

O Send us a ray of divine light to enlighten our understanding, so that, freed from the darkness of human ignorance, we may contemplate heavenly things.

✠ Let us ask the Lord with tender hearts and burning love to purify and adorn our souls, so that we deserve to be the dwelling of his body in the sacrament of the Eucharist.

• A gift so precious as to give all other gifts their worth.

✠ To approach such a sacrament, a mystery so divine, it is only right that love arrives arrayed in fear.

• To see you in the Eucharist, I must believe what is counter to what I see.

✠ At such a token of love, my soul dissolves and my heart, moved with tenderness, sheds tears of joy.

• May we participate in your generosity.

✠ O gracious gift! Who could know you sufficiently to know how to thank you!

• Fix in our souls your virtues and the love of your precious Son.

✠ Let us receive and conceive him perpetually in our souls so that we may attain the promise of eternal bliss.

O Grant us the gift of not only speaking but of knowing and loving the eternal truth that is God, in whom we will delight for all eternity.

✠ Divine grace, you are the soul's greatest gift! Embrace me!

Fourth Sunday in Lent

Gracious Father, whose blessed Son Jesus Christ came down from heaven to be the true bread which gives life to the world: Evermore give us this bread, that he may live in us, and we in him; who lives and reigns with you and the Holy Spirit, one God, now and for ever. *Amen.*

*S*or (Sister) Juana Inés de la Cruz was a writer of tremendous versatility and intellect, who expressed her deep love for the Blessed Virgin and the Holy Eucharist in poetry, morality plays, and theological discourses.

Nobel laureate Octavio Paz called Sor Juana the first great poet of the Americas. "There was nothing ordinary about her person or her life," he said. "She was exceptionally beautiful, and poor. Abruptly she gives up worldly life and enters a convent—yet, far from renouncing the world entirely, she converts her cell into a study filled with books, works of art, and scientific instruments, and transforms the convent locutory into a literary and intellectual salon."

Juana was born to unmarried parents in a village outside of Mexico City around 1650; her father is believed to have been a Basque soldier and her mother of Mexican heritage. She was a child prodigy who learned to read at the age of three and taught herself Latin and the Aztec language Nahuatl, as well as mathematics, astronomy, philosophy, and theology from books in her grandfather's library. At the age of eight, she went to live with a wealthy aunt in Mexico City; at sixteen, she went to work as a lady in waiting for the wife of the Mexican viceroy.

In 1667, when she was nineteen, she professed an "aversion to marriage" and entered the order of the Discalced Carmelites, but after two years moved the Convent of Santa Paula, joining the more lenient Order of Saint Jerome, where she professed her vows in 1669. There, through her writing, she became a celebrated scholar, amassing a large library and a collection of musical and scientific instruments.

The 1680s were an especially prolific time for Sor Juana, who took Teresa of Ávila as her self-proclaimed mentor. Juana wrote poetry, plays, and devotional works, and she composed music and corresponded with influential leaders of church and state. She received numerous commissions for poetry, hymns, and liturgical dramas to meet the ecclesial needs of churches and religious communities in Mexico City, Puebla, and Oaxaca. Her poetry and other writings were widely read in Spain, where she had many admirers. She is said to have been the most widely published poet of the Spanish Empire during her time; her collected works cover many volumes and comprise more than 2,000 pages.

In 1690, the bishop of Puebla published, without Sor Juana's knowledge or permission, a letter of hers that criticized the sermon of a Jesuit preacher. The bishop entitled her letter *Carta Artenagó* (*Letter Worthy of Athena*) and assigned the pseudonym Sister Filotea to the writer, admonishing her to give up writing and devote herself to prayer and other religious duties. In response, Sor Juana published the *Respuesta a Sor Filotea de la Cruz,* in which she strongly defended a woman's right to knowledge and education as necessary prerequisites to understanding theology and Holy Scripture.

As penance for her perceived attack on church authority, and in order to avoid official censure, Sor Juana was silenced. She was compelled to stop writing and forced to sell her 4,000-volume library (believed by some to be the largest private library in the Americas at the time) and musical instruments. In addition, she was assigned to work in the convent's infirmary. During a serious epidemic—possibly of plague—the following year, Sor Juana became ill while providing care to her sisters, and died. Mexico has honored Sor Juana by putting her image on its currency.

Sor Juana is commemorated in the Anglican Communion on April 18.

This prayer is taken from Sor Juana's *Devotional Exercises for the Nine Days Before the Feast of the Most Pure Incarnation* and her play *The Divine Narcissus.* The illustration is based on the image of Sor Juana found on Mexico's 100-peso bank note.

MARY OF EGYPT

Monastic (born ca. 344–died 421)

If you, O Lord, should mark iniquities, Lord, who could stand? But there is forgiveness with you, so that you may be revered.

—Psalms 130:3–4

✝ Blessed is God Who cares for the salvation of all people and their souls.

O May God defend us from the evil one and from his designs, for fierce is his struggle against us.

✠ When I reflect on the evils from which Our Lord has delivered me, I have imperishable food for hope of salvation.

• I am fed and clothed by the all-powerful Word of God.

✠ God does not desire the death of a sinner but magnanimously awaits our return to Him.

• Truly, O Lord, Thou dost not forsake those who seek Thee!

✠ The Word of God which is alive and active, by itself teaches us knowledge.

• Lead me by the hand along the path of repentance!

✠ O Blessed Virgin, thou hast shown me thy great love for all people; glory to God Who receives the repentance of sinners through thee.

• The Mother of God helps me in everything and leads me by the hand.

✠ For the sake of the Incarnate Word of God, pray to the Lord for me who am such a sinner.

O Blessed is God Who has shown me how He rewards those who fear Him.

✝ May God Who works amazing miracles and generously bestows gifts on those who turn to Him with faith, reward those who seek light for themselves in this story.

Fifth Sunday in Lent

Almighty God, you alone can bring into order the unruly wills and affections of sinners: Grant your people grace to love what you command and desire what you promise; that, among the swift and varied changes of the world, our hearts may surely there be fixed where true joys are to be found; through Jesus Christ our Lord, who lives and reigns with you and the Holy Spirit, one God, now and for ever. *Amen.*

*T*he life of Mary of Egypt teaches us of the transformational power of repentance and that God's grace can be found in the sanctity of our own interior wilderness.

Mary was born in rural Egypt to a wealthy Christian family in approximately 344. She ran away from home at the age of twelve to the bustling city of Alexandria, where she sought unrestrained sexual pleasure, taking special delight in seducing pilgrims. She refused to accept money for sex, supporting herself by spinning flax and begging.

After seventeen years, she joined a group of pilgrims bound for Jerusalem. Once in Jerusalem, she attempted to follow the pilgrims into the Church of the Holy Sepulcher, but an invisible force blocked her from entry. Realizing that her own sinfulness was preventing her from entering the church, Mary wept and repented of her sins before an icon of the Blessed Virgin. She was then able to enter the church, and, upon beholding a relic of the True Cross, committed her life to God. Returning to the icon, she heard a voice telling her enter the desert.

Mary, after washing her face and hands in the waters of the Jordan, crossed the river in a small boat and entered the desert, surviving for forty-seven years on three loaves of bread, whatever plants she could find and "the all powerful Word of God" alive and acting in her life. For the first seventeen years she wandered the desert hills, tormented by thoughts and temptations from her past life. When her clothes wore out, she endured the summer heat and winter cold of the desert.

Zosimus was a monk in a desert monastery where each Lent, the brothers would fast in the desert. He had been wandering in the desert for twenty days when he glimpsed a figure in the distance. Zosimus pursued the furtive figure who called out to him by name, explaining that she was a woman and had no clothes. She asked for his cloak to use as a covering. She then told Zosimus her story, begging him not to share the story while she remained alive. She asked him to return the following year on Maundy Thursday to bring her the Holy Eucharist.

The following year, on Maundy Thursday, Zosimus put the elements of the Eucharist in a basket and set out to meet her, as they had agreed. At the appointed spot, Zosimus saw Mary on the opposite bank of the river. Mary made the Sign of the Cross and walked over the surface of the river to Zosimus. When Mary reached Zosimus, she asked for a blessing and requested that he recite the Creed and the Lord's Prayer before administering the Holy Eucharist to her. After she partook of the Holy Mysteries, she raised her hands to the heavens and said, "Lord, now let your servant depart in peace, for my eyes have seen your salvation." Her final request was that Zosimus go back to his monastery and return in a year to the spot of their first meeting.

When Zosimus returned according to her request, he found Mary lying dead next to a message in the sand asking that her body be buried. The ground was too hard for Zosimus to dig, but he looked up and saw a friendly lion, which he asked to dig her grave. After Mary was buried, Zosimus returned to the monastery and he told his fellow monks all that had happened. It is said that Mary died in the year 421.

The feast of Mary of Egypt is celebrated on April 1 by the Roman Catholic Church, and on April 3 in the Anglican Communion; in the Orthodox church she is remembered on April 1 and again on the fifth Sunday of Lent.

This prayer is taken from the account of Saint Sophronius. The illustration is based on a French woodcut from the Wellcome Collection. Mary is depicted with long, flowing hair, which may indicate confusion with Mary Magdelene. In the Middle Ages the "sinful woman" mentioned in the seventh chapter of the Gospel of Luke was conflated with the two Marys to form an archetype of the reformed and repentant prostitute.

DAMIEN OF MOLOKAI

Priest and Missionary (1840–1889)

Let the same mind be in you that was in Christ Jesus, who, though he was in the form of God, did not regard equality with God as something to be exploited, but emptied himself, taking the form of a slave.

—Philippians 2:5–7

☩ Let us place all our hope and center all our desires in Heaven.

O The voice that has called us to make a generous sacrifice of all is the voice of God Himself.

✠ Let us be in the hands of God as tools in the hands of a skillful workman.

• Let us persevere in the service of God.

✠ Let us walk on in the ways of holiness and justice.

• It is Jesus Christ who directs all our steps.

✠ May God strengthen me and give me the grace of perseverance.

• All I desire is to accomplish the holy will of God.

✠ All that God does is right.

• How good God is.

✠ Pray that we may have courage to fulfill the holy will of God, everywhere and at all times.

O We are in the hands of an all-powerful God Who has taken us under His protection.

☩ Whether in life or death, we belong to Jesus.

Almighty and everliving God, in your tender love for the human race you sent your Son our Savior Jesus Christ to take upon him our nature, and to suffer death upon the cross, giving us the example of his great humility: Mercifully grant that we may walk in the way of his suffering, and also share in his resurrection; through Jesus Christ our Lord, who lives and reigns with you and the Holy Spirit, one God, for ever and ever. *Amen.*

Father Damien exemplifies the suffering servant, lovingly giving his life for those whom he served.

Damien was born in Flemish Belgium in 1840, the youngest of seven children born to a corn merchant and his wife, who were devout Catholics. As a young boy, Damien enjoyed playing with lambs, earning him the nickname "the little shepherd." Inspired by his mother's reading from the *Lives of the Saints,* young Damien and his brother once skipped school to play "hermits."

When he was eighteen, Damien, who studied for a career in business, often prayed late into the night to know God's will for him. On Christmas Day 1858, Damien discerned a call to join his older brother Pamphile as a member of the Society of the Sacred Hearts of Jesus and Mary. He entered the order, taking the name of a third-century physician and martyr. Damien was admitted as a lay brother, but with additional instruction from Pamphile, he was sent to Paris to train for the priesthood.

After hearing the bishop to the Sandwich Islands (now Hawai'i) preach on Easter Sunday 1861, Damien began praying to an icon of Saint Francis Xavier, the Apostle to the Indies, for his intercession to become a missionary. Two years later, his brother Pamphile was set to sail for mission work in the Sandwich

Islands, but was struck with typhus. Damien petitioned the Superior General of the Order for permission to take his brother's place, and after a hastily arranged farewell visit to his parents, Damien set sail for Hawai'i, learning English *en route.*

Damien arrived in Honolulu in 1864, where he was ordained a priest. For nine years, Damien served as the priest for up to seven churches in the Puna district of Hawai'i, traveling between them on horseback and on foot. He used his meager personal income and his skills as a carpenter to build four new chapels and restore another, while bringing salvation to hundreds of souls through baptism. He wrote to his parents, "I am very happy in the office which the Lord has entrusted to me."

Leprosy, or Hansen's disease as it is now called, was introduced to Hawai'i in the 1830s, and the disease spread quickly. King Kamehameha V signed an act allowing government officials to arrest and confine persons with the illness. Those with advanced cases were forcibly relocated to one of two settlements on an isolated peninsula of the island of Moloka'i.

In 1873, at the age of thirty-three, Damien, who had learned to speak both English and Hawai'ian, volunteered to be the resident priest for the 800 residents of the leper colony on the Kalaupapa peninsula of Moloka'i. As soon as he set foot on the island, he realized that this would be his life's work. Initially, he slept under a tree in the open air until he could build himself a small house. With the help of the residents, he also built a water system, a chapel, an orphanage, and more than three hundred small cottages with simple furniture for the residents. He demonstrated to the residents the value of their lives by honoring their deaths: making their coffins and building a fence around the graveyard.

Although his religious superiors had admonished him never to touch the residents or eat with them, he nursed the sick, bandaged their sores, shared bowls of poi, and smoked pipes with them. "I make myself a leper with the lepers, to gain all to Jesus Christ," he wrote to his brother Pamphile.

In December 1884, Damien began showing symptoms of the disease, but continued his priestly duties, saying, "I have accepted this malady as my special cross." Mother Marianne Cope, who came to Kalaupapa to assist him, cared for Damien in his last year. Damien died in 1889 and was laid to rest under the same tree where he first slept when he arrived on Moloka'i.

The feast day for Father Damien in the Roman Catholic Church is May 10; in the Anglican Communion he is commemorated with Marianne Cope on April 15.

This prayer is taken from Damien's letters to his family. The drawing is based on a photograph of Damien taken in the last year of his life.

ÓSCAR ROMERO

Archbishop and Martyr (1917–1980)

So if you have been raised with Christ, seek the things that are above, where Christ is, seated at the right hand of God.

—*Colossians 3:1*

✞ The transcendence that the church preaches is a transcendence from the human heart. And from the very heart of misery to transcend it, to elevate it, and to say to them, "You are valuable."

○ Let us not tire of preaching love; it is the force that will overcome the world.

✞ Here there is a challenge from Christ to the goodness of humankind. It is not enough to be good. It is not enough to not do evil.

• The ones who have a voice must speak for those who are voiceless.

✞ We suffer with those who have disappeared, those who have had to flee their homes, and those who have been tortured.

• There are many things that can only be seen through eyes that have cried.

✞ Peace is not the product of terror or fear. Peace is not the silence of cemeteries. Peace is the generous, tranquil contribution of all to the good of all. It is right and it is duty.

• Peace is the product of justice and love.

✞ Let us truly live the beauty and responsibility of being a prophetic people.

• We are workers, not master builders; ministers, not messiahs. We are prophets of a future that is not our own.

✞ Our persecution is nothing more nor less than sharing in the destiny of the poor.

○ We know that every effort to better society, especially when injustice and sin are so ingrained, is an effort that God blesses, that God wants, that God demands of us.

✞ I do not believe in death without resurrection. If they kill me, I will rise again in the people of El Salvador. If God accepts the sacrifice of my life, then may my blood be the seed of liberty and the sign that hope will soon become a reality.

The Resurrection of the Lord

O God, who for our redemption gave your only-begotten Son to the death of the cross, and by his glorious resurrection delivered us from the power of our enemy: Grant us so to die daily to sin, that we may evermore live with him in the joy of his resurrection; through Jesus Christ your Son our Lord, who lives and reigns with you and the Holy Spirit, one God, now and for ever. *Amen.*

Saint Óscar Romero, a man of peace, was killed for his solidarity with the poor. He calls us to bring the redemption of Christ into the world through transformation of the heart.

Born in 1917 in Ciudad Barrios, El Salvador, Óscar was baptized into the Roman Catholic Church. In his youth, he was apprenticed to a carpenter, but at the age of thirteen, he announced that he wanted to be a priest. Upon graduation from the national seminary in San Salvador, he completed his theological studies at the Gregorian University in Rome, where he graduated *cum laude* and was ordained a priest in 1942. Óscar remained in Rome to work on a doctoral degree, but was summoned home to El Salvador by his bishop, due to a shortage of priests.

Back home in El Salvador, Óscar served as a parish priest for twenty years, later becoming the rector of a seminary and directing a conservative newspaper for the archdiocese. In 1970, he was consecrated a bishop, and was assigned to an impoverished diocese. As a bishop, Óscar's motto was *Sentir con la Iglesia,* or "Feel with the Church," expressing the imperative for the Church to see the agony of the passion in the oppression of the poor, who are the body of Christ.

In 1977, Óscar was appointed archbishop of San Salvador, during a time of great political instability. The junta government and the wealthy elite considered the soft-spoken, conservative bishop a safe choice who would be their ally.

The Resurrection of the Lord

During Óscar's tenure as archbishop, he experienced a profound spiritual transformation that was catalyzed by the Salvadoran military's assassination of his dear friend and fellow Jesuit, Father Rutilio Grande, three weeks after Óscar's installation. When Óscar heard of the killing of Fr. Grande and his companions, he had their bodies brought back to lie in state at the cathedral in San Salvador. The funeral Mass at the cathedral in San Salvador was attended by 100 priests and an immense crowd that spilled outside of the cathedral.

After the funeral, Óscar took four bold steps to bring attention to the gravity of the murders and the oppression of the poor: (1) he refused to participate in any governmental functions until Fr. Grande's murderers were brought to justice; (2) he published a notice of excommunication for "the authors of the crime"; (3) he called for schools to be recessed for three days of reflection; and (4) in consultation with priests and religious in the archdiocese, Óscar canceled all Masses throughout the country the following Sunday except for a *Misa Unica* that would take place on the steps of the cathedral and be broadcast throughout the country.

More than 100,000 people filled the plaza outside of the cathedral that Sunday. In his sermon, Óscar declared that "anyone who attacks one of my priests, attacks me." Through his weekly homilies that were broadcast throughout the country, he became the voice of the voiceless. On March 23, 1980, his sermon specifically appealed to the soldiers in the army and members of the national guard, "Brothers, you belong to our own people . . . Do not kill! No soldier is obliged to obey an order counter to the law of God."

In his homily at Mass the next day, he preached, "Those who surrender to the service of the poor through love of Christ, will live like the grain of wheat that dies..." He returned to the altar, when, during the elevation of the Host, a lone gunman stepped into the open door of the church and fired a single bullet into his heart. He completed his life as he had lived it, with authenticity and in solidarity with the poor. Those responsible for Romero's murder were never brought to justice.

The Resurrection of the Lord

The feast day for Óscar Romero is celebrated on March 24 by the Roman Catholic Church and the Lutheran Church; he is commemorated by the Anglican Communion, along with the martyrs of El Salvador on the same day.

This prayer is taken from Óscar Romero's sermons and radio addresses. The illustration is based on an undated photograph of him greeting worshipers in San Salvador.

The Resurrection of the Lord

MARIA SKOBTSOVA

Monastic, Social Reformer,
Theologian, Poet (1891–1945)

In this you rejoice, even if now for a little while you have had to suffer various trials,
so that the genuineness of your faith—being more precious than gold that, though
perishable, is tested by fire—may be found to result in praise and glory and honor
when Jesus Christ is revealed.

—*1 Peter 1:6–7*

✟ "Let us love" means not only unity of the mind but also of action—it means life in common.

O Love of God—that is the chief and only thing. All the rest is just obedience.

✟ Each person is the very icon of God incarnate in the world.

• The way to God lies through love of people.

✟ In our love for our neighbor we are united with Christ.

• Love is not a thought but an activity.

✟ We receive the poor in the name of Christ, because we are aflame with his sacrificial love.

• One can love sacrificially only in the name of Christ.

✟ Whoever gives, receives; whoever impoverishes himself, gains in wealth.

• Christianity is collaboration with God.

✟ The cross of Christ is the eternal tree of life, the union of heaven and earth.

O The crucified Christ gave his flesh to be crucified, suffered in his human soul, gave his spirit into the hands of the Father.

✟ He calls us to do the same. Love to the end and without exception.

Almighty and everlasting God, who in the Paschal mystery established the new covenant of reconciliation: Grant that all who have been reborn into the fellowship of Christ's Body may show forth in their lives what they profess by their faith; through Jesus Christ our Lord, who lives and reigns with you and the Holy Spirit, one God, for ever and ever. *Amen.*

Mother Maria Skobtsova is a penitent for modern times whose life embodies the second great commandment.

Born in 1891 to a devout and aristocratic Orthodox family, Maria grew up in Anapa, a small Russian village on the Black Sea. After her father died when Maria was fourteen, she became an atheist, unable to believe that a just God would allow an unjust death.

Maria and her mother then moved St. Petersburg, Russia, where Maria was drawn to groups advocating radical social change. When she was eighteen, Maria married a fellow writer and social revolutionary, but they divorced three years later, while she was pregnant. Her passion for social justice led her back to Jesus, whom she saw a heroic historical figure. While in St. Petersburg, Maria studied briefly at the Theological Academy, its first female student; she also published two volumes of poetry.

After the outbreak of the Russian Revolution in 1917, Maria and her mother returned to Anapa, where Maria served as its deputy mayor. Here, Maria's faith began to deepen and she married again, but the young family soon had to flee Russia and the Bolsheviks.

Two more children were born as the family emigrated across eastern Europe, finally settling in Paris in 1923. There they lived in extreme poverty with other

Russian refugees and Maria became involved with the Russian Student Christian Movement, where she served as a social worker in the Russian community. In winter 1926, her daughter Anastasia contracted meningitis and died after a one-month hospitalization, during which Maria kept a daily bedside vigil. This death marked a turning point in her life; out of this tragic loss, Maria entered into a new expansive form of motherhood, embracing "all who need maternal care, assistance, or protection."

In Paris, Maria continued publishing poetry and religious writings. She worked tirelessly to provide for the needs of the growing community of Russian émigrés, yet remained unsure of her vocation. Her bishop suggested that she consider becoming a nun, developing a new form of "monasticism in the world"; Maria was professed as a nun in 1932, at the age of forty.

With financial help from her bishop, Maria organized a house to serve the needs of the poor. She soon moved to a larger property that provided housing for several dozen women. She converted the stable to a chapel adorned with icons and embroidery of her own creation, established a part-time school, and served 100 meals daily to the poor and needy. In 1939, she was joined by the priest, Father Dmitri Klépinin, who was to become an invaluable partner. Mother Maria visited Russians in mental health institutions, serving as a translator for the doctors and securing discharges for many who had been confined.

During the Nazi occupation of Paris in 1940, Mother Maria opened the doors of the house to Jewish families. She worked with Fr. Dmitri to provide falsified baptismal certificates to help Jews avoid deportation to concentration camps. She brought food to Jews detained by the Nazis and smuggled Jewish children out of internment camps, hiding them in garbage cans which sympathetic municipal workers transported to safety. In spring 1943, she was arrested by the Gestapo and transported to the Ravensbrück concentration camp.

According to Holocaust survivors, Mother Maria was greatly loved by her fellow prisoners and was a source of great encouragement. She willingly shared her food rations with others, even as her own health declined. She was murdered in the gas chambers on Holy Saturday 1945, shortly before the camp was liberated.

The feast day for Maria Skobtsova is July 20 in the Eastern Orthodox Church; in the Anglican Communion she is commemorated on July 21.

This prayer is taken from the translated essays of Mother Maria Skobtsova. The illustration is based on an undated photo.

MECHTHILD OF HACKEBORN

(1241–1298)

Mystic and Theologian

They said to each other, "Were not our hearts burning within us while he was talking to us on the road, while he was opening the scriptures to us?"

—*Luke 24:32*

✞ Glory to you, O sweetest, noblest, resplendent, ever-tranquil, and ineffable Trinity.

O I pray that my every thought, speech, action, and desire may be guided today according to the good pleasure of your gracious will.

✞ I commend my inner and outer sight to divine wisdom, asking God to give me the light of knowledge to discern his will and everything that pleases him.

• O only sweetness, I beg you to abide with me.

✞ I commend my hearing to divine mercy, asking God to give me understanding of all that I will hear this day.

• The word of God gives life to the soul, infusing it with spiritual joy.

✞ I commend my mouth and voice to divine fidelity, asking God give savor to everything I should utter this day.

• I praise, worship, magnify, glorify, and bless you, good Jesus.

✞ I commend my heart to divine love, asking God to draw it into his own heart with all delight and kindle it in his love.

• I offer you my heart like a blossoming rose.

✞ Holy Father, in a union of love with your loving Son, I commend to you my spirit.

O I confess with all my heart and voice, I praise and I bless; to you be glory forever.

✞ O gentle Lamb, have mercy on me.

O God, whose blessed Son made himself known to his disciples in the breaking of bread: Open the eyes of our faith, that we may behold him in all his redeeming work; who lives and reigns with you who lives and reigns with you, in the unity of the Holy Spirit, one God, now and for ever. *Amen.*

Through the luminous spirituality of Mechthild of Hackeborn and her radiant visions, we are granted a glimpse of the divine splendor as we experience the risen Christ.

Mechthild, born in 1241, was a daughter of the noble and influential Thuringian family of the baron of Hackeborn-Wappra and his wife. At birth, Mechthild's health was so precarious that her parents rushed her to the local priest, fearing that she might die unbaptized. After baptizing her, the priest prophesied that Mechthild would "become a saintly religious woman in whom God will work wonders."

When Mechthild was seven years old, her mother took her to visit her older sister Gertrude, who was a nun at a nearby nunnery. Mechthild was so taken with the experience that she begged to stay with her sister. Her parents, recognizing the workings of grace, yielded to her entreaties and allowed her to remain. Young Mechthild was a gifted student and advanced quickly in her studies and piety.

In 1251, Gertrude was elected abbess of the monastery, which soon moved to a new location in Helfta, adjacent to her family's estate. Under Gertrude's leadership the abbey became a center for learning and scholarship; Mechthild and the other young nuns were given a rigorous education in the liberal arts and had a high degree of Latin literacy; they read the works of Bernard of Clairvaux, Augustine, and others.

Third Sunday of Easter

Mechthild was much beloved by her sisters for her cheerful demeanor, humility, and piety. As she grew in the faith, Mechthild was given charge of young children who were put in the abbey's care, and she was made headmistress of the convent school. In this capacity Mechthild became the spiritual mother of a five-year-old child named Gertrude, who would later be known as Saint Gertrude the Great.

Because of her exquisite and richly spiritual singing voice, Mechthild was known within her religious community as "God's nightingale." She served as the abbey's choir mistress, leading them with great zeal. For Mechthild, sung prayer was a pathway to deepened devotion.

Mechthild's innate musical lyricism also found voice through her visions. Although she began experiencing visions at the age of seven, she kept them a secret for most of her life. It was only during a severe illness during her fiftieth year that Mechthild disclosed them to Gertrude the Great and another nuns who, at the abbess Gertrude's direction, committed them to writing. These visions became known as the *Liber Specialis Gratiae,* or the *Book of Spiritual Grace,* and was widely disseminated and read in the years after her death.

Mechthild's visions were deeply grounded in the liturgical life of the religious community at Helfta, which became the setting for the manifested presence of Christ. In describing her visions of the risen Lord, Mechthild used highly poetic language to convey her clairvoyant and clairaudient visions of mystic espousal, which included vivid colors, gemstones, musical instruments, hymns, and sung prayer.

The feast day for Mechthilde of Hackeborn in the Roman Catholic Church is November 19; she is commemorated in the Anglican Communion on November 21, along with Gertrude the Great.

This prayer is taken from Mechthild of Hackeborn's *Book of Special Grace.* The illustration is based on a nineteenth-century woodcut on paper from the National Museum in Krakow. I suspect that in the original, the bird was intended to represent the Holy Spirit, but I drew it with the more pointed beak of a nightingale, because I enjoyed the ambiguity.

Third Sunday of Easter

SOJOURNER TRUTH

Mystic, Preacher, Social Reformer
(1797–1883)

Even though I walk through the darkest valley of the shadow of death, I fear no evil;
for you are with me; your rod and your staff-they comfort me.

—*Psalms 23:4*

☦ God is from everlasting to everlasting.

O God is the great house that will hold all his children; we
   dwell in him as the fishes in the sea.

   ☦ God is all over. There is no place where God is not.

   • I know I am a servant of the living God.

   ☦ Lord, what wilt thou have me to do?

   • God's holy purpose must be fulfilled.

   ☦ The Spirit calls me and there I must go.

   • I have learned from Jesus to suffer and forgive.

☦ This is Jesus! Praise, praise, praise to the Lord.

• Jesus will walk with me through the fire and keep me from harm.

☦ The Lord shall go with and protect me.

O The Lord has been good; he has given me business to do, and has moved me to do it.

☦ Be a follower of the Lord Jesus.

O God, whose Son Jesus is the good shepherd of your people: Grant that when we hear his voice we may know him who calls us each by name, and follow where he leads; who, with you and the Holy Spirit, lives and reigns, one God, for ever and ever. *Amen.*

*D*uring her lifetime, it was said that Sojourner Truth carried "a tongue of fire, but a heart of love," preaching the Gospel to all who would listen.

Sojourner Truth was born into slavery in rural New York in 1797, the eleventh child of James and Elizabeth "Mau Mau" Baumfree. When she was a young girl, her mother taught her the Lord's Prayer and told her to tell her cares to God, "who will always hear you and help you." As a child, she was bought and sold four times to enslavers who physically and sexually abused her. As a teenager, she prayed daily at a sanctuary she created for herself under a willow tree, telling her troubles and sufferings to God.

Sojourner gave birth to five children between 1815 and 1826: one died in childhood, one fathered by her enslaver John Dumont, and three fathered by Thomas, to whom she was married. When John Dumont failed to grant her freedom in 1826 as he had promised her, Sojourner stayed to complete the seasonal work, then left the premises with her infant daughter Sophia in one arm and a small parcel of food and clothes in the other. She heard the voice of God direct her to walk to freedom, leaving just before daybreak. After walking five miles carrying Sophia, the Lord guided Sojourner to the house of the Van Wagenens, an abolitionist Quaker family. They paid Dumont $20 to ensure her freedom until she would be emancipated by New York State law in 1827.

While living with the Van Wagenens, Sojourner had a life-changing vision in which Jesus appeared to her "radiant with love," revealing the omnipresence of God and calling her to repentance; he appeared to her as great and powerful and "altogether lovely." She experienced Jesus as a "friend through whom love flowed, as from a fountain"; he became her "soul-protecting fortress." With financial help from local Quakers, in 1828 Sojourner successfully sued for the return of her son Peter, who had been illegally sold to a plantation in Alabama. She saw her victory in this case as clear evidence of answered prayer, and in the process became one of the first Black women to legally prevail at court against a White man.

In 1829, Sojourner and Peter, now emancipated, moved to New York City, where she found work as a housekeeper and became an active member of the Methodist Church; her daughter Sophia remained with the Van Wagenens. In the early 1830s Sojourner became involved with a revivalist sect, whose leader she was later falsely accused of murdering. Acquitted of the murder, Sojourner prevailed in a slander suit against those who had originally filed the charges.

It was on June 1, 1843, during the week of Pentecost, that Sojourner (whose given name had been Isabella) received a call from God to leave the city and "testify the hope that was in her." And it was at this time that she received the name Sojourner Truth. She explained, "The Lord gave me 'Sojourner,' because I was to travel the land; and the Lord gave me 'Truth,' because I was to declare the truth to the people." She attended revivals and began preaching from New York to Boston.

Sojourner settled briefly in Northampton, Massachusetts, where she began dictating her memoir, published in 1850 by William Lloyd Garrison. In 1851, while on a lecture tour, she gave her famous "Ain't I a Woman" speech to the Ohio Women's Convention, challenging prevailing ideas on racial and gender inferiority. In 1857, Sojourner moved to Battle Creek, Michigan, where, during the US Civil War she exhorted young Black men to join the Union Army and organized community support for the Black troops. Following the War, she was invited to the White House, where she met with President Abraham Lincoln. She died in Michigan in 1883, attended to by her two daughters. Her last words were, "Be a follower of the Lord Jesus."

Sojourner Truth is commemorated in the Anglican Communion on July 20.

The words of this prayer are taken from *The Narrative of Sojourner Truth,* which she dictated to Olive Gilbert. The illustration is based on a drawing by Robert Jackson and a photograph in the National Archives.

GEORGE HERBERT

Priest and Poet (1593–1633)

Jesus said to him, "I am the way, and the truth, and the life. No one comes to the Father except through me. . ."

—*John 14:6*

✠ Come, my Joy, my Love, my Heart; Such a Joy as none can move:

○ Such a Love, as none can part, Such a Heart, as joys in love.

✤ Love is that liquor sweet and most divine,

• Which my God feels as blood, but I, as wine.

✤ Oh, let thy blessed sacrifice be mine,

• And sanctify this altar to be thine.

✤ For my heart's desire unto Thine is bent:

• I aspire to a full consent.

✤ I live to show his power, who once did bring

• My joys to weep, and now my griefs to sing.

✤ Come, my Way, my Truth, my Life: Such a Way, as gives us breath:

○ Such a Truth, as ends all strife: Such a life that killeth death.

✠ Let all the world in every corner sing, "My God and King!"

Almighty God, whom truly to know is everlasting life: Grant us so perfectly to know your Son Jesus Christ to be the way, the truth, and the life, that we may steadfastly follow his steps in the way that leads to eternal life; through Jesus Christ your Son our Lord, who lives and reigns with you, in the unity of the Holy Spirit, one God, for ever and ever. *Amen.*

*T*he poetry of George Herbert transforms complex theology into meaningful images, giving us new ways to comprehend the mystery of the Word made flesh. His life shows us the joy of virtue and the freedom of service to God and his people.

George Herbert, born in 1593 at Montgomery Castle, was from a prominent Welsh family; his father was a nobleman and his mother was a woman of "wisdom and virtue," and a patroness of the arts. John Donne, who was George's godfather, wrote a cycle of seven sonnets to his mother Magdalen. After the death of George's father, when George was three, his mother moved her ten children to London, where George studied at the Westminster School. An excellent student, he won a scholarship to Trinity College, Cambridge, where he read classics, excelled in music, and began writing religious poetry. He was elected public orator of the university in 1620, a position that was often a stepping stone to public office, to which he aspired, though his mother wanted him to be a priest.

In 1624, Herbert was elected to Parliament and ordained a deacon. His political career was cut short, however, by the death of King James I, who had been Herbert's supporter. Three years later he resigned his position and dedicated his learning and abilities "to advance the glory of that God that gave them." In 1628, he moved to Wiltshire to escape the plague in London; a year later he married.

Fifth Sunday of Easter

George was ordained a priest in 1630 and assigned to a small country church at Bemerton, England, outside of Salisbury. The church and rectory were in a state of disrepair, so George undertook their restoration, at his own expense. He and his wife had no children, though they adopted his three orphaned nieces, whom they raised. The family of five walked to church twice daily for morning and evening prayer. "I will labor like my Savior, making humility lovely in the eyes of all men, by following the merciful and meek example of my dear Jesus."

George served God as the rector of Bemerton, where his parishioners called him "Holy Mr. Herbert." He served at Bemerton for only three years, before dying from tuberculosis just before his fortieth birthday. When he realized that his death was imminent, George gave his longtime friend, Nicholas Ferrar, a collection of poems that he had written with the instruction that after his death they should be either burned or published, as Nicholas saw fit. Ferrar recognized the beauty and grace of the poems and published them under the title, *The Temple.* The small volume of poetry gained immediate and widespread popularity. George described his own poetry as "a picture of the many spiritual conflicts that have passed betwixt God and my soul, before I could submit mine to the will of Jesus my Master; in whose service I have found perfect freedom."

Two of his poems were put to music and became the well-loved hymns, "Teach Me, My God and King," and "Let All the World in Every Corner Sing." His poetry influenced many later poets, including Samuel Taylor Coleridge, Emily Dickenson, T. S. Eliot, Seamus Heaney, and the writer Simone Weil. Many consider George Herbert to the greatest devotional poet of the English language.

Today, George is remembered for *The Temple* and a prose volume, *The Country Parson,* intended as a pastoral care guide for ministers describing "the form and character of a true pastor" and emphasizing the importance of prayer ("God's breath in man, returning to his birth"), keeping the daily offices, Holy Scripture, the book of "infinite sweetness," and the benefits of pastoral blessings for the congregation.

Fifth Sunday of Easter

George Herbert is commemorated on February 27 by the Anglican Communion.

This prayer is compiled from his poems *The Call, The Agony, The Altar, Discipline,* and *Antiphon (I).* The image was inspired by a 1674 engraving by Robert White, now in the National Portrait Gallery, London.

HADEWIJCH OF BRABANT

Poet and Mystic
(flourished first half of the thirteenth century)

You know him, because he abides with you, and he will be in you.

—John 14:17

✟ God is marvelous in his goodness, total in his presence, rapturous in his sweetness.

O If God is yours in love, you must live for him, by yourself being love.

⳨ Live exclusively for holy Love out of pure love, in order to devote yourself to God himself in the works that please Love.

• Those who live in Love are renewed each day.

⳨ Abandon yourself to the truth that he himself is.

• Be inwardly so free that you are always longing for God.

⳨ Pray that he may give you himself to love, for he is the God of love and knows perfectly our need of love.

• Do everything with reliance on Love and live in sweet love.

⳨ Apply yourselves to the exercise of love, and adorn yourselves with the light of truth.

• The flame of love burns constantly in the very marrow of my soul.

⳨ May new light give you new ardor; new works, new delights to the fullest.

O Bear God in your heart with constant remembrance, and embrace God lovingly with an open and expectant heart.

✟ Love is everything!

O God, you have prepared for those who love you such good things as surpass our understanding: Pour into our hearts such love towards you, that we, loving you in all things and above all things, may obtain your promises, which exceed all that we can desire; through Jesus Christ our Lord, who lives and reigns with you and the Holy Spirit, one God, for ever and ever. *Amen.*

*H*adewijch is a writer of dazzling originality, whose ardent and embodied love for Christ opens a luminous portal to Divine Love.

Little is known about the life of this Flemish poet and mystic who lived near Antwerp, in the region of Brabant. Although her writing influenced John of Ruusbroec and several other religious thinkers of her era, her works fell into obscurity and no *vita* was written for her.

To understand Hadewijch's life, we look to the spiritual movement of the Beguines that began in the early thirteenth century in the Low Countries. The Beguines were financially self-supporting communities of laywomen who lived in simplicity and religious devotion, modeled after the Way of the Apostles, or *via apostolica.* Since they were not members of an established religious order, they were outside of the authority of the Church.

From her writing, it is clear that Hadewijch was highly educated: she was well versed in Old and New Testaments, the writings of Origen, Augustine of Hippo, and Bernard of Clairvaux, and other religious scholars and theologians. Similarly, her knowledge of French courtly love poetry suggests that her family was aristocratic—some scholars have suggested that she was a musician or *trobairitz,* the female form of a troubadour. Though she had excellent command of Latin and French, she chose to write in the Dutch vernacular, perhaps to make her writing more accessible to her fellow Beguines.

Sixth Sunday of Easter

Starting at age ten and continuing throughout her life, Hadewijch had intense mystical visions, which would often leave her incapacitated for days afterward.

Hadewijch became the head of a community of Beguines, guiding their spiritual formation and advocating for the care of the sick. For unknown reasons, Hadewijch was relieved of her authority and exiled from her community, though she continued to be a spiritual director for some of her followers through her letters. In her later years, she wandered the countryside, possibly associating with one of the newly emerging public hospitals. The date of her death is not known.

Although she was a master of medieval vernacular poetry and prose, her works languished in relative obscurity for nearly 800 years, before their rediscovery in the late nineteenth century. Five manuscripts, believed to comprise her entire oeuvre, have survived, which include thirty-one letters, forty-five poems in stanzas, fourteen prose visions, and sixteen poems in couplets.

The overarching theme of Hadewijch's writing is the inner journey of the soul's longing for and ascent toward God. She writes about the primacy of the experience of Love, or *minne,* the union of the soul with the divine in love, and the embodied experience of the Holy Trinity.

Hadewijch is commemorated in the Anglican Communion on April 22.

This prayer is taken from Hadewijch's letters of spiritual direction and three of her poems. The image is adapted from a woodblock print illustration of Blessed Alpaïs of Cudot from the *Nuremberg Chronicle* by Hartmann Schedel (1440–1514). In the original print, Alpaïs held a martyr's palm, which I have replaced with a writer's quill.

ANTHONY OF PADUA

Friar, Priest, Theologian, Doctor of the Church

(1195–1231)

Now they know that everything you have given me is from you; for the words that you gave to me I have given to them, and they have received them and know in truth that I came from you; and they have believed that you sent me.

—John 17:7–8

✠ Behold the Cross of the Lord! Begone all evil powers! The Lion of the Tribe of Judah, the Root of David has conquered, Alleluia! Alleluia!

O O God, send forth your Holy Spirit into my *heart* that I may perceive; into my *mind* that I may remember; and into my *soul* that I may meditate.

✠ Let us speak as the Holy Spirit gives us to speak, asking him humbly and devoutly to pour out his grace.

- Lord, may your grace ever help and correct me.
✠ Inspire me to speak with piety, holiness, tenderness, and mercy.
- God's mercy is greater than a sinner's weakness.
✠ His mercy is beautiful, broad, and precious, since it cleanses us from vice.
- May I be set afire with the fiery tongues of confession;
✠ Teach, guide, and direct my thoughts and senses from beginning to end.
- Attribute to God every good that you have received.
✠ May I be strengthened now with wisdom from on high, for the sake of your infinite mercy.

O Let us ask the Lord Jesus Christ so to pour his mercy upon us, that we may have mercy upon ourselves and upon others; that we may judge no one and forgive everyone who sins against us.

✠ May he himself graciously grant this, who is blessed and glorious for ever and ever. *Amen.*

O God, the King of glory, you have exalted your only Son Jesus Christ with great triumph to your kingdom in heaven: Do not leave us comfortless, but send us your Holy Spirit to strengthen us, and exalt us to that place where our Savior Christ has gone before; who lives and reigns with you and the Holy Spirit, one God, in glory everlasting. *Amen.*

Though Saint Anthony wanted to be a missionary, he humbly submitted to God's will, becoming a brilliant preacher and theologian.

Anthony of Padua was born in Lisbon, Portugal, in about 1190; tradition holds that he was born on the Feast of the Assumption. He came from a devout and family of moderate means who sent him to the local cathedral school when he was eight. At fifteen, he entered the local Augustinian Canons Regular at St. Vincent's Monastery. After two years, Anthony received permission to transfer to the monastery of Santa Cruz in Coimbra, where he studied Scripture for eight years, and was probably ordained.

In 1220, the relics of five martyred Franciscan missionaries were brought to Coimbra from Morocco. Inspired by their zeal and faith, Anthony felt a strong calling to mission, praying, "Ah, would that the Most High might deign to let me share the crown of his holy martyrs." It was not possible for a Canon Regular to serve as a missionary, so Anthony requested permission to join the Franciscan Order, where "evangelization of the infidels" was part of their Rule. Reluctantly, this permission was granted. The following day, Anthony received the Franciscan habit.

Anthony joined a small group of friars living at the recently established hermitage of Santo Antão dos Olivais. Soon Anthony was on his way to Morocco to enlighten the Saracens. After arriving in Morocco, Anthony was struck with an incapacitating febrile illness. Hearing of his grave illness, his superior

Seventh Sunday of Easter

recalled him to Portugal, but his ship home was blown off course, landing in Messina, Sicily.

From Sicily, Anthony traveled to Assisi for the general chapter meeting of the Order, where he may have met Saint Francis. At the meeting, Anthony had hoped for an invitation to join a friary—but no one wanted the frail friar. At last, Brother Gratian, the provincial of the Romagna region of Italy, took him on as a dishwasher for the hermitage in Montepaolo. There he divided his time between communal prayer, menial chores for the brothers, and a remote cell for solitary prayer.

After Anthony had been there for about a year, there was a gathering of local Dominican and Franciscan friars. Due to an oversight, no preacher had been designated. At the last minute, the superior asked Anthony to preach. To the astonishment of the gathered friars, their "dishwasher" spoke with exceptional eloquence, revealing a great depth of theological and biblical understanding, freely quoting Holy Scripture from memory.

For the next four years, Anthony embarked on apostolic work in Italy and France as an itinerant preacher. He was renowned for bringing people whose faith had lapsed back to the Church, earning him the nickname the "Hammer of the Heretics." Toward the end of 1223, Saint Francis himself wrote Anthony a letter requesting him to teach theology to the Friars Minor in Bologna. Anthony was appointed Provincial Superior of the Franciscans in northern Italy in 1227, a post he served for four years, choosing to live in the city of Padua.

Anthony preached in and around Padua, where he drew great crowds, although the estimates of 30,000 are probably an overstatement. It is said that his presence brought about reconciliations throughout the city. In spring 1231, Anthony spent time at a hermitage in Composanpiero, but when his frail health began to fail, he asked to be taken back to Padua, where he died on the outskirts of the city.

Anthony was considered a wonder-worker during his lifetime, and many miracles are associated with his name. When a misguided novice stole his cherished psalter, Saint Anthony prayed for both the thief and the book's return.

Seventh Sunday of Easter

Finding a fierce demon blocking his path, the penitent thief returned the psalter. From this story, Saint Anthony became the patron saint of lost items.

The feast day for Saint Anthony of Padua is celebrated in the Roman Catholic Church on June 13.

> This prayer is taken from the sermons and motto of Saint Anthony. The drawing is based on an illustration found on the final page of a volume of his sermons, dated 1649.

SUNDAR SINGH

(1889–ca. 1929)

Evangelist, Teacher of the Faith

Divided tongues, as of fire, appeared among them, and a tongue rested on each of them. All of them were filled with the Holy Spirit and began to speak in other languages, as the Spirit gave them ability.

—Acts 2:3–4

✠ My Lord God, my all in all, life of my life, and spirit of my spirit, look in mercy upon me.

O So fill me with Your Holy Spirit that my heart shall have no room for love of any but You.

✠ God is a Spirit, and to see God and God's Spiritual Kingdom we must be born of that Spirit.

• The baptism of the fire of the Holy Spirit is necessary to purify the soul.

✠ God so pours the Holy Spirit into the life of the prayerful that they become "living souls."

• Prayer is communion with God, the giver of all good gifts.

✠ Our prayers, kindled by the fire of the Holy Spirit, rise up to God, overcoming sin and evil, and return to earth filled with God's blessings.

• I seek no other gift but You, who are the Giver of Life and all its blessings.

✠ When the spiritual eyes are opened, then you can surely see Him who is Spirit.

• The one who lives in nearness to God readily hears his voice.

✠ No harm will come to us if God's Spirit, the life of our life, dwells in us, and if we keep our lives clean by daily prayer.

O Take away from my heart all that is opposed to You, and enter and abide and rule for ever.

✠ May I serve God who has saved me by grace.

Almighty God, on this day you opened the way of eternal life to every
race and nation by the promised gift of your Holy Spirit: Shed abroad
this gift throughout the world by the preaching of the Gospel, that it
may reach to the ends of the earth; through Jesus Christ our Lord, who
lives and reigns with you, in the unity of the Holy Spirit, one God, for
ever and ever. *Amen.*

Sundar Singh preached with the fire and power of an apostle, bringing
the message of Jesus Christ to the people of Tibet.

Sundar Singh was born to a wealthy Sikh family living in the northern
Indian village of Rampur in 1889. His mother was a devout woman who
encouraged young Sundar to memorize Sikh and Hindu religious texts and
regularly took him to see a local *sadhu,* or holy man, for religious training.
Although he attended the local Presbyterian Mission School, Sundar saw
Christianity as a "false religion," and threw stones at Christians preaching in
the marketplace. Though he was faithful to his own religion, he received no
satisfaction or peace from its observance.

After the deaths of Sundar's mother and brother in 1904, fourteen-year-old
Sundar became severely depressed. In his anger, he burned a copy of the New
Testament, page by page. Three days later, in the depths of his despair, he prayed,
"O God, if there is a God, show me the right way or I will kill myself," intending
to lay his head on the railway track when the morning train passed by. While
he was praying, he saw a human form appearing inside a great light. Expecting
to see Krishna, he instead saw Jesus Christ, radiating glory and love, saying,
"How long will you persecute me? I have come to save you." Sundar repented of
his past behavior and was immediately flooded with a feeling of immeasurable
peace. This moment of conversion was the turning point in Sundar's life.

The Day of Pentecost

When he told his father that he was now a follower of Jesus and wanted to be baptized, his entire family renounced him and cast him out of the family home; that night he slept under a tree, but was warmed by the joy in his heart. The missionaries at his school arranged for Sundar to attend a Christian boarding school in another village. In 1905, on his sixteenth birthday, he was baptized by Anglican missionaries; he committed himself to preaching the Gospel of Jesus Christ, not as an ordained priest, but as an Indian *sadhu,* dressed in a saffron robe and turban; wandering and teaching among the people of India and Tibet. Although Sundar briefly received formal schooling in theology at an Anglican seminary in India, he left after a year, because he found the training ill-suited for his calling as a Christian *sadhu.*

Between 1908 and 1923, Sundar made numerous trips into Tibet on foot to preach the Gospel. Once, he was arrested and brought before the local lama, who sentenced him to be thrown into a dry well which would be covered and locked. For three days he languished at the bottom of the well, amid the decomposing corpses of his predecessors. On the third night, he heard the lid of the well being opened. A rope was let down, which he grasped with his remaining strength and was pulled up to safety. Once to the surface, he looked for his rescuer, but saw no one. Sundar resumed preaching in town and was once again arrested and brought before the lama. Initially enraged that someone had stolen the key to the well, he was dumbfounded to find the well's only key still in his possession. The lama then banished Sundar from the city.

Sundar gradually widened his ministry, traveling to southern India, Sri Lanka, Burma, Singapore, Malaysia, China, and Japan. As his fame grew, he traveled to Europe, Scandinavia, the United States, and Australia between 1920 and 1923. After many years of ascetic living, Sundar's health began to deteriorate and he focused on writing, producing six short volumes between 1925 and 1927. His greatest joy during this period was his reconciliation with his father, who converted to Christianity.

Yet Sundar still longed for Tibet. In April 1929, Sundar once more set out for Tibet by foot, with plans to return by mid-June. When no one had heard from him by July, two friends retraced his route, but found no one who had seen him. The details of his death remain a mystery. Sundar, like Enoch, "walked with God; then he was no more, because God took him" (Gen 5:24).

Sundar Singh is commemorated in the Anglican Communion on June 19.

This prayer is taken from the collected works of Sadhu Sundar Singh. The illustration was drawn from a photograph taken in 1926.

ATHANASIUS OF ALEXANDRIA

Theologian, Bishop (ca. 298–373)

For we cannot do anything against the truth, but only for the truth.

—2 Corinthians 13:8

✞ Light, radiance, and grace are *in* the Trinity and *from* the Trinity.

O When we share in the Spirit, we possess the love of the Father, the grace of the Son and the fellowship of the Spirit himself.

✟ The Father makes all things through the Word and in the Holy Spirit.

• In this way the unity of the holy Trinity is preserved.

✟ The Son is everywhere; for he is in the Father and the Father in him.

• The Son of God became man so that we might become God.

✟ The Spirit is not outside the Word, but, being in the Word, through him is in God.

• He who receives the Spirit is called a temple of God.

✟ The Trinity is a wholly creative and energizing reality.

• We acknowledge the Trinity, holy and perfect.

✟ Worship the Father, confessing the Son and in him the Spirit.

O For the Spirit is inseparable from the Son, as the Son is inseparable from the Father.

✞ Let us kneel with true hearts and worship Him truly and His holy cross, for He is the Lord of all.

Almighty and everlasting God, you have given to us your servants grace, by the confession of a true faith, to acknowledge the glory of the eternal Trinity, and in the power of your divine Majesty to worship the Unity: Keep us steadfast in this faith and worship, and bring us at last to see you in your one and eternal glory, O Father; who with the Son and the Holy Spirit live and reign, one God, for ever and ever. *Amen.*

We remember Athanasius for his unwavering defense of the divinity of Jesus Christ and trinitarian doctrine against the Arian heresy.

Athanasius, whose name means "without death," was born to an Egyptian family of moderate means, between 295 and 299, possibly to Christian parents; he grew up during the the Diocletian persecution, which was especially severe in Egypt. When the bishop of Alexandria met him, young Athanasius was pretending to baptize a friend of his; the bishop was so impressed with his "liturgy," that he did not rebaptize the child.

At the age of twenty-three, Athanasius, who was intelligent and largely self-taught, was ordained a deacon serving Alexander, bishop of Alexandria, then one of the three most influential sees in Christendom. It was about this time that he wrote his first major treatise, *Against the Heathen,* in which he defends Christian doctrine. In 325, the Roman emperor Constantine convened the Council of Nicaea, the first worldwide council of the Church, to bridge growing divisions within the Church. For two months, some 300 bishops met, striving for consensus to resolve the intensely divisive theological dispute now known as the Arian heresy. Arius, a charismatic presbyter from Libya with a large following, believed that Christ was created by the Father, and thus was not coeternal with Him and not "of one being with the Father," which led to his excommunication.

Trinity Sunday

In 328, three years after the Council of Nicaea, Bishop Alexander died and was succeeded by Athanasius. He was so young at the time of his consecration that some challenged whether he had attained the minimum age allowed by canon law. Athanasius led the Alexandrian Church during times of great trial and controversy, as the fragile consensus of Nicaea began to crumble and followers of Arius gained influence with Roman emperors.

Arius was able to gain favor with the emperor Constantine, who ordered Athanasius to restore him to full fellowship with the church. When Athanasius refused, Constantine exiled him from Alexandria. Over the course of his forty-six-year episcopacy, Athanasius was exiled five times by four different emperors, for a total of seventeen years, prompting him to say, "If the world is against truth, then I am against the world," giving rise to the epitaph "Athanasius against the World."

Athanasius made good use of his time in exile, sending pastoral letters to his flock in Alexandria and writing several important works. Many scholars believe he wrote *On the Incarnation,* which some have called the defining text on Nicene theology, during his first exile in Trier, Germany (then part of Gaul). His second exile was spent mostly in Rome during a time of growing conflict between the Eastern and Western Church and infighting and political turmoil within the Roman Empire.

The ten years between second and third exiles (346–356) were among his most fruitful, and he first met Saint Anthony of Egypt. Athanasius spent his third and fourth exiles in the Egyptian desert, writing *The Life of Antony,* which inspired many to the ascetic life and monasticism. His last exile was spent in the suburbs of Alexandria, possibly taking refuge among the tombs of his ancestors. Throughout his five exiles, Athanasius had the unwavering support of Egyptian Christians.

Athanasius returned to Alexandria from his fifth and final exile in 366, when he was about seventy years old, and he spent his remaining time promoting Church unity. His Festal Letter of 367 provides the first record of the complete listing of the twenty-seven books in the New Testament canon. "No one may add to them, and nothing may be taken away from them," he said. Athanasius died in 373, having reconciled with most of his earlier enemies.

The feast day of Saint Athanasius is celebrated throughout the Church: on January 18 in the Eastern Church and on May 2 in the Western Church.

This prayer was taken from the following writings of Athanasius: *On the Incarnation, Letters to Serapion, On the Trinity,* and *The Life of Antony.* The illustration was inspired by references to Athanasius as "the black dwarf" and by icons of Abba Moses the Black.

Trinity Sunday

LOUISE DE MARILLAC

Vowed Religious, Social Worker (1591–1660)

Happy are they whose way is blameless, who walk in the law of the Lord. Happy are they who keep his decrees, who and seek him with their whole heart. . . .

—Psalms 119:1–2

✢ You are my God and my All. I recognize you and adore you, the one true God in three Persons, now and forever.

O What I am unable to do on account of my powerlessness or other obstacles in me, God will do by his kindness and omnipotence.

✤ Is there anything more excellent in heaven or on earth than the treasure of the Holy Spirit?

• O Eternal Light, lift my blindness! Create in me simplicity of being.

✤ The practice of charity is so powerful that it gives us the knowledge of God.

• We are called to imitate Christ and to serve Him in the person of His poor.

✤ Do the little you can very peacefully and calmly to allow for the guidance of God in your lives.

• I desire no other satisfaction but that of loving and willing God's good pleasure.

✤ Renew your confidence in God and abandon yourself to His guidance.

• The grace of my God will accomplish whatever He pleases in me.

✤ I must abandon myself entirely to His providence to be completely His.

O We must persevere our souls in peace and await, with joy, the coming of Our Lord whom we must desire as the beloved of our souls.

✢ I am, in the love of Jesus Crucified, your humble servant.

Remember, O Lord, what you have wrought in us and not what we deserve; and, as you have called us to your service, make us worthy of our calling; through Jesus Christ our Lord, who lives and reigns with you and the Holy Spirit, one God, now and for ever. *Amen.*

The life of Louise de Marillac reveals a legacy of charity in which love of God and love of neighbor are interpenetrated; where service to the poor is service to Jesus.

Born near Paris in 1591, Louise de Marillac was the out-of-wedlock child of a French nobleman and an unknown mother. In infancy, Louise was sent to the Royal Abbey of Poissy and placed under the care of her aunt, a Dominican sister; there she was educated at the convent school in the arts, Latin, and Holy Scripture. She was removed from the school after her father's death, when Louise was about twelve, and was sent to a *pension,* or boarding house, where she learned domestic skills including cooking, sewing, care of the sick, and household management. Louise's childhood was marked with loneliness; she was rarely without "some occasion of suffering."

At the age of twenty, Louise requested to enter a Capuchin order, but was refused due to her frail health. When she was twenty-two, her uncle arranged for her to marry an aristocrat; in twelve years of marriage, the couple had one son. Louise became a leader of the Ladies of Charity, an organization of wealthy women dedicated to assisting those suffering from poverty and disease, though she never gave up her desire for a religious vocation. During the last four years of their marriage, Louise provided bedside care for her husband, who had developed a chronic illness, probably tuberculosis, and died in 1625.

On the Feast of Pentecost, 1623, when her husband was very ill, Louise received a *lumière,* or "gift of light"; a powerful vision in which her mind was

Sunday Closest to May 11—Proper 1

"instantly freed of all doubt" and she understood that she was called to live in community and serve the poor and sick, guided by a new spiritual director. This vision was a turning point in her life: she pronounced a vow of widowhood after her husband's death, committing herself to the service of Christ in the poor, especially the sick poor and poor children. This became the new focus of her life. It was not long after this that Vincent de Paul became her spiritual director, a relationship that would be of great mutual benefit.

The seven years following her husband's death formed a period of transition and transformation, serving as an unofficial novitiate, in which Louise made a self-professed "Act of Consecration," offering herself to God. She became increasingly active with Vincent's Confraternity of Charities, and the two worked closely together, providing care for the sick and the poor. Louise's *lumière* would finally come to fruition in 1633, when she and Vincent established the Daughters of Charity, the first noncloistered religious institute of women devoted to active charitable works.

Louise devoted the final twenty-seven years of her life to the formation and leadership of the Daughters of Charity. The charism of this community was to serve the poor, especially the sick, in the communities where they lived. Louise directed the formation of the Daughters, whom she saw as her spiritual children, educating them and guiding them in the imitation of Christ. The group received ecclesial approbation in 1655 and was placed under the jurisdiction of the bishop of Paris. The Daughters were laywomen who took simple annual vows, distinguishing them from the canonically religious. In addition to serving the poor in their houses, the Daughters established homes for foundling infants, administered hospitals, ministered to galley slaves, and started *petites écoles,* or "little schools," to educate poor children. Under Louise's vision and leadership the Daughters grew from a small group of four women living together in her own home, to more than sixty houses of service at the time of her death in 1655. Today there are more than 13,000 Daughters serving in ninety-six countries throughout the world.

Sunday Closest to May 11—Proper 1

The feast day for Louise de Marillac is celebrated in the Roman Catholic Church on March 15; in the Anglican Communion she is commemorated on that day, together with Vincent de Paul.

This prayer is taken from the collected writings of Louise de Marillac. The illustration is based on engraved likeness of Louise from the seventeenth century.

PATRICK OF IRELAND

Bishop and Missionary (ca. 390—ca. 461)

In you, O Lord, I take refuge; let me never be put to shame. In your righteousness deliver me and rescue me; incline your ear to me and save me.

—Psalms 71:1-2

✚ I will tell of the Great blessings God has granted to me.

O We should praise him and proclaim his kindness to everyone in the world.

✚ We worship one God in three parts by the sacred name of the Trinity.

• Because of my faith in the Trinity, I must not worry.

✚ I turn with my whole heart to the Lord my God, because nothing is impossible for him.

• There is no other God—there never was and there never will be.

✚ God took care of me on my journey, and I wasn't afraid.

• With kindness and strength he rescued me.

✚ God came along and with his power and compassion raised me up.

• God made me into someone who can care about others and work to help them.

✚ I must give thanks to my God continuously. He has helped me to keep my faith through difficult times.

O I am not afraid because I know Heaven waits for me. I throw myself on the mercy of God, who is in charge of everything.

✚ You must understand—because it is the truth—that it was all the gift of God.

Almighty and merciful God, in your goodness keep us, we pray, from all things that may hurt us, that we, being ready both in mind and body, may accomplish with free hearts those things which belong to your purpose; through Jesus Christ our Lord, who lives and reigns with you and the Holy Spirit, one God, now and for ever; *Amen.*

*B*eyond the blarney and green beer lies the real person of Patrick, who responded faithfully to God's call to serve the people of Ireland, combining a life of contemplation with forceful action.

Patrick, born around 390 in the western part of Roman Britain, was a third-generation Christian—the son of a deacon and the grandson of a priest. His family was of the landowning aristocracy, providing Patrick with an education that included literacy in Latin and basic mathematics. As a teenager, he turned away from the faith and described himself as an atheist. At the age of fifteen he committed a serious crime, the memory of which haunted him his entire life; historians have speculated that he may have killed someone.

When Patrick was sixteen his family villa was attacked by Irish raiders. Patrick was captured and later sold as a slave to a chieftain in northern Ireland, for whom he tended sheep. Patrick later wrote, "God used this time to shape and mold me into something better." He arose before sunrise to say a hundred prayers in the morning and said another hundred at night. He began fasting as an act of purification, and his love for God grew.

After six years of tending sheep, Patrick had two prophetic dreams. In the first, a voice told him, "Soon you will be going home." The next night he heard the voice again, saying, "Behold, your ship is ready." He fled his enslaver, heading southeast for some 200 miles, finding the ship that took him back to Britain. Patrick and the ship's captain and crew landed in an unpopulated part of Britain. The group wandered in the British wilderness for two weeks and were near starvation when the captain challenged Patrick's God to provide for the group. Patrick confidently asserted that God would provide abundant food to fill their bellies; that very afternoon a large herd of swine crossed them, which the crew slaughtered and ate their fill.

After returning to Britain, Patrick made his way back to his family homestead where he received another vision in which he heard "The Voice of the Irish" calling him back to walk among them. "He who gave his life for you, he it is who speaks within you." Patrick made the decision to return to evangelize Ireland.

Little is known about Patrick's training for holy orders. Tradition holds that he was taught and ordained in Gaul by Saint Germanus, the bishop of Auxerre, and that he received his commission in Rome from Pope Celestine. His autobiography includes only a cursory mention of travel "through Gaul, Italy, and the islands of the Tyrrhenian Sea."

In 432, Patrick succeeded Palladius as Ireland's second bishop, Palladius having served less than one year. Patrick moved with skillful diplomacy among the local Irish kings and chieftains, offering gifts to gain their favor and protection. Patrick had great success, especially among marginalized people, ministering to enslaved Christians who had been brought to Ireland; he also found Irish women, including daughters of Irish nobility, to be open to the message of the Gospel.

The extant writings of Patrick include his autobiographical *Confessio,* and an epistle to the soldiers of the British tyrant Coroticus, who had captured and killed a band of Christian converts, still dressed in white from their recent baptism.

Many colorful stories, mixing metaphor and legend, are associated with Patrick. The story of his driving the snakes from Ireland probably refers to vile sorts of humans, rather than reptiles. The prayer commonly called the Lorica (a *lōrīca* is a piece of armor that shields the heart), or Saint Patrick's Breastplate, is often attributed to Patrick but was probably written a century after his death—though it may reflect his reliance on prayer in times of danger and his love of the Holy Trinity.

After a lifetime of service, Patrick died on March 17, 461, in Saul, Ireland, the place where he had built his first church.

Saint Patrick is celebrated throughout the Church on March 17.

This prayer is taken from the *Confessio* of Saint Patrick. This drawing is based on an illustration from *Faeth Fiadha: The Breastplate of Saint Patrick* (Dolmen Press, 1957).

ALCUIN OF YORK

Deacon (ca. 730–804)

Think of us in this way, as servants of Christ and stewards of God's mysteries.

—*1 Cor. 4:1*

☦ O God of light, praise becomes you always from heart and lips, that we may love you, the Holy One, always and forever.

O Grant me the wings of faith that we may fly upwards to you.

☦ Eternal and supreme wisdom, scatter the darkness of our ignorance.

• Kindle us and make us vessels worthy of spiritual light.

☦ May God protect and defend us without, and strengthen and confirm us within.

• Eternal goodness, deliver us from evil.

☦ May the hand of the Lord be our helper, and his holy arm grant us help all the days of our lives.

• Eternal power be our support.

☦ May Christ alone be to you light and life and the beauty of salvation.

• Eternal and supreme light, shine in my heart.

☦ Grant us to love simplicity and purity, and always to seek after those things that make for peace.

O Teach us faith, awaken hope, and fill us with love: O blessed Trinity.

☦ Grant that we may always seek to see your face.

Grant, O Lord, that the course of this world may be peaceably governed by your providence; and that your Church may joyfully serve you in confidence and serenity; through Jesus Christ our Lord, who lives and reigns with you and the Holy Spirit, one God, for ever and ever. *Amen.*

Alcuin blended his heart and intellect in service to God. Beloved friend to many and advisor to Charlemagne, he was a revered scholar, theologian, educator, and liturgist.

Alcuin was born in Yorkshire in 735, the son of a noble family related to Saint Willibrord, Apostle to the Frisians. As a child, he was tutored in the liberal arts at the renowned cathedral school in York, where he later became a teacher and headmaster. He believed a rigorous education was fundamental to the understanding of spiritual teaching. Alcuin was ordained to the diaconate in 770, at a time when scholarship and teaching were important aspects of a deacon's ministry.

Alcuin visited Rome three times; while in Italy in 781 he met Charlemagne, king of the Franks, who recognized Alcuin's intellect and scholarship and invited him to become part of his court in Aachen. There he would advise the king on matters of education and religion and become head of the royal palace school. Alcuin was the foremost scholar of the Carolingian Renaissance, called "the most learned man anywhere to be found." He taught Charlemagne's own sons, bringing the legacy of English scholarship from Venerable Bede to the revival of Western learning under Charlemagne, thus making the palace school at Aachen a center of medieval learning and culture.

In 796, Charlemagne appointed Alcuin to be the abbot of St. Martin's Abby in Tours, which allowed him to live the contemplative life he had long desired. He was also appointed abbot at three other abbeys, attracting scholarly monks from across Europe. At St. Martin's, Alcuin personally oversaw the scriptorium where the Carolingian minuscule script was perfected, bringing much needed conformity and improved legibility to handwritten manuscripts. He also oversaw the revision of the Latin Vulgate, which gave the medieval Church its standard Bible text. Alcuin is credited with inventing the question mark.

Alcuin's significant influence persuaded Charlemagne to stop killing pagans who refused to be baptized, explaining that true faith is necessarily a "free act of the will." At Charlemagne's behest, Alcuin reformed the liturgy, writing and editing several collects that are still in use, including the Collect for Purity, which is said at the beginning of the liturgy for the Holy Eucharist ("Cleanse the thoughts of our hearts by the inspiration of your Holy Spirit").

A prolific letter writer, Alcuin's correspondence yields some of his best-known writings; more than 300 letters have survived. These letters were treasured by their recipients, copied, and widely shared. In his letters Alcuin demonstrates warmth, simplicity, and his commitment to a life of moderation and prayer.

Alcuin was man of paradox: he was a reformer of the liturgy, though he was never ordained a priest; and he was an abbot though he never took religious vows. He died in Tours in 804.

Alcuin is celebrated on May 19 by the Roman Catholic Church and on May 20 by the Eastern Orthodox Church and the Anglican Communion.

This prayer is taken from Alcuin's letters and prayers. The image is based on a portrait of Alcuin that was made shortly after his death. It is found in a Bible from St. Martin's Abbey in Tours.

Sunday Closest to May 25—Proper 3

FRANCIS OF ASSISI

Friar and Deacon (1181–1226)

You shall put these words of mine in your heart and soul, and you shall bind them as a sign on your hand, and fix them as an emblem on your forehead.

—*Deut. 11:18*

☦ Most High, all-powerful, all-good Lord, All praise is Yours, all glory, all honor, and all blessings.

O Praised be You my Lord with all Your creatures, especially Sir Brother Sun; he is beautiful and radiant with great splendor. Praised be You, my Lord, through Sister Moon and the stars, in the heavens you have made them bright, precious, and fair.

☦ Praised be You, my Lord, through Brothers Wind and Air, and fair and stormy,

• Praise all weather's moods, by which You cherish all that You have made.

☦ Praised be You my Lord through Sister Water,

• Praised be Sister Water, so useful, humble, precious, and pure.

☦ Praised be You my Lord through Brother Fire, through whom You light the night.

• Praised be Brother Fire, he is beautiful and playful and robust and strong.

☦ Praised be You my Lord through our Sister, Mother Earth who sustains and governs us.

• Praised be Mother Earth who produces varied fruits with colored flowers and herbs.

☦ Praise be You my Lord through those who bear sickness and trial. Blessed are those who endure in peace, by You Most High, they will be crowned.

O Praised be You, my Lord through Sister Death, Blessed are they She finds doing Your Will.

☦ Praise and bless my Lord and give Him thanks, and serve Him with great humility.

O God, your never-failing providence sets in order all things both in heaven and earth: Put away from us, we entreat you, all hurtful things, and give us those things which are profitable for us; through Jesus Christ our Lord, who lives and reigns with you and the Holy Spirit, one God, for ever and ever. *Amen.*

Saint Francis of Assisi is greatly loved for his love of animals, but his true legacy is a life that embodies the love of Christ.

Francis of Assisi was born about 1182 to a wealthy cloth merchant and his wife. As a youth, Francis, charismatic and well-liked, aspired to a life of chivalry. At the age of twenty, he joined his townsmen in a military campaign against the neighboring town of Perugia, where he was captured and held in a dungeon.

Following his release a year later, Francis had a dream in which a voice told him to "follow the master, not the servant," which he understood as a call to follow God rather than men. The turning point of this "conversion" was his chance meeting with a group of lepers outside of Assisi. Rather than avoiding them, Francis approached the lepers, spoke with them, embraced them, and gave them money. In this encounter, he was graced to see them as his fellow suffering brothers, and his life path turned away from worldly vanity and toward conformity with Christ.

In fall 1205, Francis stopped to pray in a run-down church in San Damiano, where he heard the voice of Christ speak to him from the crucifix, saying three times, "Francis, go and repair my Church." To finance the restoration, Francis sold some cloth belonging to his father, gave his proceeds to the local priest, and requested lodging in the church. His outraged father charged Francis with theft in the ecclesial court, where the local bishop ordered Francis to repay his father. Francis returned the money, renounced his inheritance, and stripped off his clothes, throwing them at his father's feet. Standing naked in the public square, he said, "No longer do I call Pietro di Bernadone my father; but now I say: 'Our Father, who art in heaven.'" Francis spent the next two years as a solitary, begging alms, rebuilding San Damiano and two other churches, and preaching in the streets.

The simplicity, sincerity, and lived truth of his message attracted local men to Francis. Initially a group of four *frati minores,* or "little brothers," the group grew to about a dozen within a year; within five years, they numbered some 5,000 friars. Francis drew up a simple Rule for them to live by and traveled to Rome to gain approval of the new order from Pope Innocent III. About this time, Francis was ordained to the diaconate.

In 1212, in cooperation with Saint Clare, Francis founded the Second Order, known as the "Poor Clares," who followed the rigorous Franciscan standards of simplicity and poverty that Francis espoused. In addition, the Third Order of Penitents, or tertiaries, was established for the men and women who wanted to bring Franciscan ideals to the broader community.

In summer 1219, during the Fifth Crusade, Francis and another friar traveled to Damietta, Egypt, to promote universal brotherhood. When his words went unheeded, Francis and his companion set out for the camp of the Egyptian leader, where the Sultan al-Kamil, a man known for his spirituality, received them graciously. The meeting lasted for several days; after the encounter, the sultan ordered that Francis be returned safely to the Christian encampment.

In 1224, Francis moved to the mountain village of La Verna, where he lived in a hermitage. As he was praying on the Feast of the Holy Cross, he saw a vision of the crucified Christ with six wings, like a seraph, filling him with joy and sorrow at the sight of his crucified Lord. In this mysterious moment, he received the *stigmata:* wounds began to appear on his hands and feet, as though pierced through by a nail, and his right side began to ooze with blood, a culmination of a life lived in imitation of Christ.

In his later years, Francis suffered from both debilitating illness and searing eye pain, which forced him to move back to his monastery. He surrendered to "Sister Death" on October 3, 1226.

The feast of Saint Francis is celebrated on October 4 throughout the Western Church.

This prayer is a modification of *Canticle of Brother Sun and Sister Moon,* the first known use of poetry in the Italian language. The illustration is inspired by a 1925 woodcut by Giorgio Wenter Marin.

CHARLES WESLEY

Priest (1707–1788)

Go and learn what this means, 'I desire mercy, not sacrifice.' For I have come to call not the righteous but sinners.

—Matthew 9:13

☩ Come, thou almighty King, help us thy Name to sing, help us to praise.

O Father whose love unknown, all things created own, build in our hearts thy throne, Ancient of Days.

☩ Come, thou long-expected Jesus, born to set thy people free;

• From our fears and sins release us, let us find our rest in thee.

☩ Visit then this soul of mine! Pierce the gloom of sin and grief!

• Fill me, radiancy divine; scatter all my unbelief.

☩ All my trust on thee is stayed; all my help from thee I bring;

• Cover my defenseless head with the shadow of thy wing.

☩ Jesus, thou art all compassion, pure, unbounded love thou art;

• Visit us with thy salvation, enter every trembling heart.

☩ By thine own eternal Spirit rule in all our hearts alone;

O By thine all sufficient merit raise us to thy glorious throne.

☩ Savior, take the power and glory; claim the kingdom for thine own.

O God, from whom all good proceeds: Grant that by your inspiration
we may think those things that are right, and by your merciful guiding
may do them; through Jesus Christ our Lord, who lives and reigns with
you and the Holy Spirit, one God, for ever and ever. *Amen.*

C harles Wesley has been called the greatest hymn writer of all time; the
profound theology of his hymns continues to inspire.

Charles Wesley (the younger brother of John Wesley), was born in England
in 1707, eighteenth child of Anglican priest Samuel Wesley and his wife Susanna.
His mother spent an hour with each of her children every week, instructing
them in the way of the faith. When he was eight, Charles went to London to live
with his eldest brother and attend the Westminster School, where he became a
King's Scholar and later head boy.

In 1727, Charles entered Christ Church College at Oxford and soon became
"lost in diversions," including a rumored affair with an actress. In his second
year, he had his first spiritual awakening, inspired by the writing of Thomas à
Kempis. He organized a group of students, later dubbed the "Holy Club," which
adopted a strict "method" of devotion and study. When his elder brother John,
an Anglican priest, returned to Oxford in 1729, he provided needed leadership
for the "Oxford Methodists," who sought to revive the practices and spirituality
of the early church. Charles remained in Oxford and received his master's degree
in 1733, hoping for a career as a scholar.

After the death of their father in 1735, John persuaded Charles to sail with
him to the American colony of Georgia, where they would serve as chaplains,
arranging for Charles to be the personal secretary for Governor James Oglethorpe.
Charles was ordained a deacon the following Sunday, and a priest the following
week. The brothers sailed for Georgia two weeks later. During a fierce gale that

ripped their ship's mainsail, a group of Moravians on board calmly sang hymns, impressing Charles with the strength imparted by congregational singing, which at that time was not a major component of Anglican worship.

Things did not go well for Charles in Georgia. He proved to be an unpopular chaplain and an incompetent secretary. To make matters worse, malicious rumors were spread (though later recanted) that Charles was having an affair with a married woman. His relationship with Governor Oglethorpe soured, and within three months, Charles was on his way back to England.

Charles arrived in England exhausted and discouraged; several bouts of ill-health followed. On Pentecost Day 1738, while convalescing in the home of a Moravian in London, Charles had a personal encounter with the Holy Spirit—he felt a heartfelt conviction that Christ had died for him *personally;* three days later, his brother John had a similar conversion. He became an open-air evangelist, preaching to crowds sometimes numbering more than 10,000 people.

In 1749, at the age of forty-one, Charles married Sally Gwynne with John serving as celebrant. Starting around 1756, Charles withdrew from active preaching to focus on his family life, but he had left his mark on Anglican and Methodist hymnody. For fifty years, he wrote ten lines of poetry a day, writing the words to nearly 7,000 hymns (some say 9,000!), including such favorites as *Hark! The Herald Angels Sing, Christ the Lord Is Risen Today!, Love Divine, All Loves Excelling,* and many others still sung today. Though Charles's sermons have largely been forgotten, he was a remarkable preacher in his own right, nearly as famous during his lifetime as his brother John.

A rift later developed between the brothers regarding the future of the Methodist movement. Charles saw Methodism as a reform movement within the Church of England, and disapproved of actions leading to separation from the Church, most especially John's unilateral decision to ordain Methodist ministers.

Charles Wesley died in 1788 at the age of eighty. It is reported that on his deathbed, he told his rector "I was brought up, I ministered, and I die in the Church of England. I pray you bury me in the churchyard." He is buried at St. Marylebone Church.

Sunday Closest to June 8—Proper 5

Charles Wesley, along with his brother John, are commemorated in the Anglican Communion on March 3.

This prayer is taken from the hymns of Charles Wesley; the illustration is inspired by an engraving by Sir William Hamilton.

CATHERINE OF SIENA

Religious Tertiary, Mystic, Doctor of the Church
(1347–1380)

So Moses came, summoned the elders of the people, and set before them all these words that the Lord had commanded him.

—*Exodus 19:7*

✠ O eternal Truth! Fragrance above every fragrance! Compassion beyond all compassion! Justice beyond all justice!

O O Love immeasurable, the Church is founded in your Son's blood and in her that blood is preserved.

✠ Set our hearts ablaze and plunge them into this blood so that we may more surely conceive a hunger for your honor and the salvation of souls.

• Holy Spirit, inflame my heart and unite it to yourself!

✠ O Fire ever blazing! High eternal Trinity, you are the measureless fire of charity.

• Warm me, inflame with Your dear love, and every pain will seem light.

✠ Boundless love! In your light I have seen light; in your light I have come to know the light.

• What a marvelous thing, that even while we are in the dark we should know the light!

✠ In love, you drew us out of yourself, giving us being in your own image and likeness.

• You have drawn me to yourself in unutterable love.

✠ Our sin lies in nothing else but in loving what you hate and hating what you love.

O Purify my soul, most high God, and listen to your servant who is calling out to you.

✠ Grant us, most kind and compassionate Father, your gentle and eternal benediction. Amen.

Keep, O Lord, your household the Church in your steadfast faith and love, that through your grace we may proclaim your truth with boldness, and minister your justice with compassion; for the sake of our Savior Jesus Christ, who lives and reigns with you and the Holy Spirit, one God, now and for ever. *Amen.*

*C*atherine of Siena, a young uneducated woman, spoke truth to power, influencing popes and politicians to do the will of God.

Catherine was the twenty-fourth child born to a Sienese wool dyer and his wife in 1347. Catherine was a devout child who taught herself the *Angelus* at age five and, when going up the stairs in her house, would often kneel on each step to say an *Ave Maria*. When she was six, she saw a vision of Christ in the sky flanked by Peter, Paul, and John. The Lord gave her a blessing, and from that moment on, she resolved to live a saintly life.

When Catherine was fifteen, her parents urged her to marry her late sister's widower. But Catherine had taken a private vow of perpetual virginity, and cut off her hair in defiance. Three years later, in 1365, she was accepted into the Mantellate, a precursor to the Third Order of the Dominicans. She lived in silent solitude, devoting herself to prayer and penance in a cell-like room at her parents' house. When Catherine was twenty-one, she experienced a mystical marriage to Christ in which the Lord placed a ring on her finger, saying, "I, your Creator and Savior, espouse you in the faith." He further told her to leave the solitude of her cell and enter a life of public service.

Emboldened by Christ's charge, Catherine began performing acts of charity throughout Siena, providing care to the poor, the sick, and the imprisoned. During the famine of 1370 and the plague epidemic of 1374 when many fled Siena, Catherine personally cared for the sick and dying at their bedsides. In addition, she ministered to prisoners, especially those condemned to death, often accompanying them to the gallows.

By 1374, Catherine's reputation for holiness became so widespread that she attracted large crowds to hear her speak and was followed by a dedicated *famiglia* of men and women whom she called her spiritual children. In fact, so many were converted by her preaching and example that additional priests were enlisted to handle the numerous confessions. It was at this time that Catherine began a prolific letter-writing campaign advocating for clergy reform, a new crusade to unite the Church, and the return of the papal residence from Avignon to Rome.

In 1375, Catherine traveled to Pisa, where she convinced leaders of two prominent city-states not to join the antipapal league. It was in Pisa that Catherine received the stigmata, though out of humility she requested that they remain visible only to herself. The following year, she was invited to Florence to help advocate with the pope that the city be released from interdict, and the faithful again be allowed to receive the sacraments.

Catherine and her entourage walked from Siena, Italy, to Avignon, France, to meet with Pope Gregory XI and personally exhort him to return to Rome. She boldly wrote him that, "Since Christ has given you authority, and you have accepted it, you ought to be using the power and strength that is yours. If you don't intend to use it, it would be better, and more in God's honor and the good of your soul, to resign . . . Cursed be you, for time and power were entrusted to you and you did not use them." Catherine wrote the pope at least fourteen times.

When she returned to Italy, Catherine founded a women's monastery outside of Siena, and began dictating an account of her mystical experiences, now referred to as *The Dialogue of Divine Providence,* or more simply, *The Dialogue.* She lived to see Pope Gregory XI's return to the Holy See in Rome and spent the last months of her life there, having been summoned by Gregory's successor, Urban VI. By this time Catherine, whose body had been severely weakened by more than a decade of extreme fasting, spent most of her time in prayer, attended by a few faithful "daughters." She died in Rome in 1380 at the age of thirty-three. In addition to *The Dialogue,* more than 380 of her letters and twenty-three prayers have been preserved.

The feast day for Catherine of Siena is celebrated throughout the Western Church on April 29.

This prayer was taken from the prayers of Catherine of Siena. The illustration is based on an undated woodcut from the Penn Libraries.

SOPHRONY OF ESSEX

Monastic, Archimandrite (1896–1993)

Everyone therefore who acknowledges me before others, I also will acknowledge before my Father in heaven.

—Matthew 10:32

✝ The Name of God is a vessel full of fragrance; a priceless gift to us from on high.

O Calling on the Name of Jesus fills our whole being with the presence of God.

☦ The Name Jesus is the channel through which divine strength comes to us.

• Invoking the Name of Jesus unites us with God.

☦ Love toward Christ, filling our whole being, works a radical change in us.

• It is essential to love him whom we invoke.

☦ Unless we labor to keep his commandments, we call upon his Name in vain.

• He who truly loves Christ will devote his whole strength to obeying his word.

☦ The Divine Spirit draws the heart to compassion for all creation.

• God calls to us, and waits for us with love.

☦ Our prayer becomes like a shaft of light focused on the dark places of our inner life.

O Offered in humility, our prayer unites heart and mind.

✝ O, Son of God, save us and thy world.

O Lord, make us have perpetual love and reverence for your holy Name, for you never fail to help and govern those whom you have set upon the sure foundation of your loving-kindness; through Jesus Christ our Lord, who lives and reigns with you and the Holy Spirit, one God, for ever and ever. *Amen.*

Saint Sophrony had a deep and abiding love of the Holy Name of Jesus. He especially loved the Jesus Prayer, "Lord Jesus Christ, Son of God, have mercy on me, a sinner," whose words are easily learned, but whose faithful application, from the depths of one's being, requires a lifetime of dedicated practice.

Born in 1896 to Orthodox parents in Tsarist Russia, his given name was Sergei Symeonovich Sakharov. He grew up in a large Orthodox family, one of eight children. From early childhood, he demonstrated a deep capacity for prayer, praying for up to an hour at a time; during these sessions, he first experienced the Uncreated Light of God. He was a talented artist and studied first at the Academy of Arts from 1915 to 1917 and later at the Moscow school of Painting, Sculpture, and Architecture in 1920 and 1921, where he used painting to reveal the eternal beauty of the created world and explore "new horizons of being."

Sophrony was deeply affected by the suffering of World War I. He fell away from his Orthodox upbringing and explored the teaching of Eastern religions. For about eight years he practiced Buddhist meditation. In 1922 Sophrony fled the Bolsheviks, traveling through Italy and Germany before settling in Paris, where he exhibited his paintings at the Salon d'Automne in 1923, and the following year at the Salon des Tuilleries. During the week of Easter 1924, he again experienced the Uncreated Light and the eternal nature of Christ himself.

The following spring, he enrolled in the St. Sergius Theological Institute but discontinued his studies when he felt called to enter a monastery.

At the age of twenty-nine, seeking deeper unity with God, Sophrony traveled to Mount Athos in Greece, the holy site of twenty Orthodox monasteries. There he entered the St. Panteleimon Monastery where he was tonsured and took the name of Sophrony; four years later, he was ordained to the diaconate. He became the spiritual son of his elder, Silouan the Athonite, and studied under him for eight years. Following Silouan's death, at his teacher's instruction, Sophrony went to live as a hermit in the Athonite desert, where he lived for six years from 1939 to 1945, during which time he was ordained into the priesthood. While living as a hermit, Sophrony became the confessor and spiritual father to many of the monks at the monastery of St. Paul; this ministry later expanded to include other Athonite monasteries.

In 1947, after twenty-two years on Mount Athos, Sophrony asked for a blessing to return to Paris to write a biography and edit the writings of his spiritual father, Silouan, which he published the following year. Many years of asceticism and privation took a heavy toll on Sophrony's health, and following a difficult surgery and nearly three months in the hospital, Sophrony, in failing health, went to live in a Russian home for the elderly on the outskirts of Paris. As his health slowly improved, people began to seek out Sophrony for spiritual guidance; in time, Sophrony's disciples implored him to establish a new monastic community.

In 1958, an English translation of Sophrony's book on Silouan was published; the following year, English benefactors acquired a property in Essex, England, on which to build the Monastery of St. John the Baptist. The original community included Sophrony and six monks and nuns; Sophrony himself, recalling his earlier days as a painter, created the icons that adorn the monastery. While at the monastery, the elder Sophrony revised and expanded his works on Silouan and published several books of his own teachings, including the spiritual autobiography *We Shall See Him as He Is.* Sophrony died in England in 1993 at the age of ninety-seven, having commended the monastery to the protection of the patriarch of Constantinople.

Saint Sophrony was canonized by the Ecumenical Patriarchate of Constantinople in 2019; his feast day in the Eastern Orthodox Christian Church is July 11.

This prayer is compiled from Saint Sophrony's book, *His Life Is Mine*. The image was drawn from a photograph taken when Sophrony was in his early nineties.

MARIE OF THE INCARNATION

Monastic, Educator (1599–1672)

Whoever gives even a cup of cold water to one of these little ones in the name of a disciple—truly I tell you, none of these will lose their reward.

—*Matthew 10:42*

☩ The love and life of Jesus be your sanctification and salvation!

O God is good and merciful everyplace in the world toward those who wish to love and serve him.

☦ Oh my divine Love, I recognize you as my great God.

• You delight me, O my Savior.

☦ My soul is absorbed in the immense and infinite grandeur of the Majesty of God.

• O eternity, beauty, goodness, love, my center, my beatitude, my all!

☦ I have no more words at the feet of the divine Majesty.

• I must be purified by dying constantly to myself.

☦ Change my life into your life; change what I am into what you are.

• My God, my God, be blessed, O my God.

☦ The soul loves and relishes only the imitation of Jesus Christ in his hidden life.

O My heart is in peace through the mercy of our good Jesus for whom we labor.

☩ While we wait for help, we remain in the pure providence of God.

Almighty God, you have built your Church upon the foundation of the apostles and prophets, Jesus Christ himself being the chief cornerstone: Grant us so to be joined together in unity of spirit by their teaching, that we may be made a holy temple acceptable to you; through Jesus Christ our Lord, who lives and reigns with you and the Holy Spirit, one God, for ever and ever. *Amen.*

*M*arie of the Incarnation exemplifies contemplation in action, a true mystic and missionary who established the first school for girls in the New World.

Marie was born in 1599 to a master baker and his wife who lived in Tours, France. One night when she was seven, she dreamed that Jesus took her in his arms, kissed her, and asked her, "Will you be mine?" Marie felt her heart enveloped by his love and answered, "Yes!" When she awoke, she felt a strong inclination to prayer and scriptural study that continued throughout her life.

When she was fourteen, Marie wanted to enter a convent, but her parents didn't approve. Instead, when she was seventeen, they arranged her marriage to a silk merchant. Her husband died two years later, leaving Marie with a six-month-old son. Marie and her son moved in with her parents, where she spent her time in prayer and meditation, supporting herself with her embroidery.

Marie went to live with her sister and her husband, where she helped manage their household. As her talent for household management grew, she soon began helping her brother-in-law with his business matters, though she longed for a religious vocation. In 1620, Marie had a mystical vision resulting in what she described as a "conversion" experience in which she personally experienced the mystery of the Holy Trinity.

In 1631, Marie entered the Ursuline monastery in Tours, having entrusted her son to the care of her sister, who raised him as her own. She described the separation from her son, then eight, as "a living death," and although she experienced severe depression in her early years, she remained certain of her vocation. She professed her vows in 1633. Shortly after Christmas 1634, Marie had another profound dream in which an unknown woman pointed her to a vast forested land, which later discernment revealed to be Canada, where she was to "build a house for Jesus and Mary." Despite considerable institutional resistance, Marie persisted in pursuing this calling. In February 1639, a wealthy widow came to the Ursulines wishing to join a mission to Canada; Marie immediately recognized her as the woman from her dream. In May Marie and six other nuns joined a group of Jesuit missionaries and set sail for New France, arriving in Quebec City, after a three-month voyage.

The women lived together in rustic quarters. By 1643, Marie, using her business acumen, supervised the building of a convent with, true to her Ursuline calling, a boarding school for Canadian and First Nations girls, the first of its kind in North America. One night in December 1650, a fire destroyed the convent; the nuns and boarders escaped from the burning building and stood together, many barefoot in the snow, singing praises to God for their safety. Marie oversaw the construction to rebuild the convent, expanding its capacity for boarders.

Marie learned the language of the Algonquin, Huron, and Iroquois people; she wrote a catechism in Iroquois and compiled dictionaries for translating these languages into French. In 1668, she conceded that although they had provided an excellent education for the daughters of the early settlers of New France, her efforts to assimilate the First Nations children into European customs were largely unsuccessful.

The surviving writings of Marie of the Incarnation include spiritual and theological treatises and more than 1,000 letters, many to her son, who became a Benedictine monk in 1641. Her memoir, *The Relation of 1654,* and an earlier autobiographical work written in 1633, provide rich detail of everyday life in

New France. During her time in the Canadian colony, Marie endured many physical hardships, including debilitating pain in her knees, failing eyesight, and possibly gout. Marie died in Québec City at the age of seventy-two. She is one of only two women represented with a statue on the façade of the Québec parliament.

The feast day for Marie of the Incarnation in the Anglican Church of Canada and the Roman Catholic Church is April 30.

This prayer was taken from the letters of Marie of the Incarnation and from *The Relation of 1654*. The illustration was inspired by a black-and-white scratchboard illustration by iconographer Julie Loneman.

MARY MACKILLOP

Monastic (1842–1909)

*They shall speak of the glory of your kingdom, and tell of your power, to make known
to all people your mighty deeds, and the glorious splendor of your kingdom.*

—Psalms 145:11–12

☦ I want with all my heart to be what God wants me to be.

O Let us belong to Him completely. He will take care
of us.

☦ He wants us to take fresh courage, to lean more on
Him and less on ourselves.

• If we have love in our hearts, we shall have God
with us.

☦ God's love is too deep for words to express.

• Be a gift of love and compassion for one another.

☦ Never see a need without doing something about it.

• Find happiness in making others happy.

☦ The Cross may press heavily, but you can be happy for all of this.

• God will carry you safely through every struggle.

☦ Work on bravely, hopefully. Do not give way to fears and anxieties.

O Believe in the whisperings of God to your own heart.

☦ All depends on prayer. Begin with it and end with it.

O God, you have taught us to keep all your commandments by loving you and our neighbor: Grant us the grace of your Holy Spirit, that we may be devoted to you with our whole heart, and united to one another with pure affection; through Jesus Christ our Lord, who lives and reigns with you and the Holy Spirit, one God, for ever and ever. *Amen.*

*M*ary MacKillop was a compassionate trailblazer, whose practical holiness and faithful perseverance call us to service.

Born in Melbourne, Australia, in 1842 to Scottish immigrants, Mary MacKillop attended local schools, but she was primarily educated by her parents. Her father had studied for the priesthood in Rome but was an inept businessman, causing the family many financial hardships. Mary would later write, "Our home . . .was a most unhappy one," though trust in God's providence remained strong. When she was sixteen, Mary was forced to work variously as a teacher, store clerk, and governess to help support her family. Mary was drawn to religious life from a young age, but there were no religious orders for women in Australia.

Mary met Father Julian Tenison Woods in 1860 and placed herself under his spiritual direction. Together, they started a school for poor children in an unused barn that Mary's brother refurbished; Mary and her sisters served as teachers for the school's fifty pupils. In 1866, Mary and Fr. Woods founded the Sisters of Saint Joseph of the Sacred Heart, with Mary becoming the first sister. At the age of twenty-four, Mary dedicated herself to God, took the religious name of Mary of the Cross and began wearing black. Fr. Woods created a Rule of Life for the sisters that was approved by the bishop in 1868. When Mary made her final profession in 1871, there were some 120 sisters managing forty-six schools, an orphanage, and a home for women needing shelter.

Political tensions within the diocese foretold difficult times ahead for the Josephite sisters. Fr. Woods had reported to the bishop that a priest within the diocese had been abusing children, and the offending priest was dismissed. Fr. Charles Horan, the best friend of the disgraced priest, swore a personal vendetta against Fr. Woods and the Josephite sisters and began a disinformation campaign to discredit them to the bishop and to make changes to their Rule of Life. Based on false information from Fr. Horan, Mary was excommunicated from the church in 1871 and the sisters were evicted from their convent. A few days before his death the following year, the bishop rescinded his order, the sisters renewed their vows and were reinvested in their habits. Mary traveled to Rome to get papal approval of the order's Rule. Mary returned with a papal decree of approval and a new constitution for the order, which was formally accepted at a General Chapter meeting where Mary was elected their first Mother General in 1875.

But more political difficulty remained as Australian bishops allied with Fr. Horan tried to exert greater authority over the order than allowed by the new constitution. Mary was banished from Adelaide and was later replaced with a new Superior General handpicked by the bishops, as they continued to make life difficult for the Josephite sisters. Throughout the many and prolonged trials and "painful circumstances" imposed by the bishops, Mary remained a model of humble obedience, setting aside any personal resentments for the greater good of the order and urging continued faith and unity among the sisters. She wrote to them that "sorrow or trial lovingly submitted to does not prevent our being happy—it rather purifies our happiness, and in so doing draws our hearts nearer to God."

After the death of the appointed Superior General in 1898, Mary was again elected to lead the order. Although she had a stroke in 1901, her mental faculties remained sharp, though she used a wheelchair for the remainder of her life. She wrote to her sisters, "Whatever troubles may be before you, accept them cheerfully, remembering whom you are trying to follow . . . Let charity guide you in all your life." Mary died in 1909; at the time of her death, there were more than 600 Josephite sisters caring for more than 1,000 needy children and adults and teaching more than 12,400 children in 117 schools.

The feast day for Mary MacKillop in the Roman Catholic Church is August 8.

This prayer is taken from the letters of Mary MacKillop. The illustration is based on a painting by Raffaele Gagliardi.

BENEDICT OF NURSIA

Monastic (ca. 480–543)

Let anyone with ears listen!

—*Matthew 13:9*

✠ Listen carefully, my child, to the master's precepts and attend to them with the ear of your heart.

O I will arise today and open my eyes to your Divine light.

☦ Each day, the Lord waits for me to translate his holy teaching into action.

• I am ready to surrender my will.

☦ In your goodness you have made me your child and I will serve you.

• May I never sadden you by my unloving actions.

☦ What is more delightful than the voice of the Lord?

• My ears will hear the call of your Divine voice.

☦ I will walk in your path with the Gospel as my guide.

• The love of Christ must come before all else.

☦ Through your power, Lord, I will do good and dwell in the shelter of your kingdom.

O May I put into practice the guidance of my Father who loves me.

✠ What is not possible by Nature, I can achieve through the help of God's grace.

O Lord, mercifully receive the prayers of your people who call upon you, and grant that they may know and understand what things they ought to do, and also may have grace and power faithfully to accomplish them; through Jesus Christ our Lord, who lives and reigns with you and the Holy Spirit, one God, now and for ever. *Amen.*

Saint Benedict of Nursia is called the father of Western monasticism. With humility he calls us to listen for the voice of God and to respond with obedience.

Nearly all of what we know about Saint Benedict comes from the writings of Saint Gregory the Great, who wrote of Benedict's life in book two of his *Dialogues,* fifty years after Benedict's death, based on information from four of Benedict's disciples. According to Gregory, Benedict was born in Norcia, in the Umbrian hills of Italy, during the declining years of the Roman Empire. When he came of age, his wealthy family sent him to Rome to study literature and law.

Disillusioned by the lewd and dissolute lifestyle, Benedict left Rome and sought a place where he could better serve God. He eventually made his way to a cave near Subiaco, east of Rome, where he lived for three years; a monk from a nearby monastery provided him with food, lowering it to the cave from above via ropes, ringing a bell to get Benedict's attention. Once during this time, when overcome with lust for a woman he knew, he ran naked through thornbushes, transforming his desire for pleasure into bodily pain.

As he grew in sanctity, Benedict was graced to perform many miracles, and his reputation for holiness grew. Monks began to seek out Benedict and place themselves under his direction. However, few could live up to his rigorous ascetic standards. Some of the monks conspired to kill him by poisoning his wine. Before drinking the wine, Benedict blessed the chalice and made the sign of the cross over it, as was his custom, at which point the vessel shattered, spilling the wine onto the ground. Benedict, correctly perceived that the wine had been poisoned, forgave the monks and gave them his blessing to seek another abbot, as he chose to return to the solitary life.

Once again, monks were drawn to Benedict, allowing him to establish twelve monasteries under his direction, each with twelve monks. A local clergyman, envious of his growing popularity, attempted to poison Benedict's bread; Benedict sensed the treachery and called upon a raven that he had befriended to dispose of the tainted loaf. Benedict moved on again, establishing a new monastery at Monte Cassino, some eighty miles south of Rome. Benedict performed many "signs and wonders" in which he discerned disobedience and sin among his monks. After the offending monk repented, Benedict would forgive him and order restitution as necessary, so that the monk would be lovingly restored to the community.

Benedict's fame continued to grow, as did his new monastery. Recognizing the need for a collective Rule of Life, Benedict wrote what is now known as *The Rule of Saint Benedict,* sometimes shortened to the *Holy Rule.* In forming his Rule, Benedict built on earlier monastic writings to form a balanced approach to communal living. In addition to the standard vows of poverty, obedience, and chastity, Benedict stressed the importance of community prayer, physical labor, and common meals: the motto of the Benedictine community is *ora et labora:* prayer and work.

Benedict died around the year 543. He had had foreseen the date of his death and ordered that his tomb be opened. The next day he was struck with a fever and died six days later "with his hands raised to heaven and breathed his last in the middle of a prayer." He is buried with his sister, Saint Scholastica—some sources say she was his twin—who also was the leader of a monastery.

Benedict is celebrated throughout the Church; his feast day is on July 11 in the Anglican Communion, the Lutheran Church, and the Roman Catholic Church, and on March 14 in the Eastern Orthodox Church.

This prayer is adapted from the prologue to the *Rule of St. Benedict*. The illustration shows the saint with a raven who, according to tradition, brought him food while he was living as a solitary.

TERESA OF LOS ANDES

Monastic (1900–1920)

I give thanks to you, O Lord my God, with my whole heart, and I will glorify your Name forever. For great is your steadfast love toward me; you have delivered my soul from the depths of Sheol.

—*Psalms 86:12–13*

✟ O Lord, make my life a canticle of love and praise.

O Let me not have any desire but to glorify God by fulfilling His will at every moment.

☩ Everything I see draws me closer to God. I feel a thirst for the infinite.

• God alone is worthy of being known.

☩ He reveals and makes himself known to souls that seek to know and love Him.

• If you give yourself to prayer, God will show Himself to you.

☩ My life is a constant prayer. Everything I do, I do out of love for my Jesus.

• I live for God alone. God is infinite joy.

☩ Place yourself and everything around you in that Heart of Jesus.

• My heart is being perfected by divine love.

☩ May Jesus find, amidst the darkness of the world, a fire of love in my pure heart.

O May the peace of Jesus reign in your soul.

✟ May Jesus be your light and life.

Almighty God, the fountain of all wisdom, you know our necessities before we ask and our ignorance in asking: Have compassion on our weakness, and mercifully give us those things which for our unworthiness we dare not, and for our blindness we cannot ask; through the worthiness of your Son Jesus Christ our Lord, who lives and reigns with you and the Holy Spirit, one God, now and for ever. *Amen.*

In Teresa of Los Andes, we see a life penetrated by the love of God and lived with joy, ardor, and complete surrender.

Teresa of the Andes was born in 1900 to wealthy and devout parents who lived on the outskirts of Santiago, Chile. Theresa was a cheerful child, interested in music and sports. The first school she attended was run by Carmelite sisters, but Teresa complained that she was bullied by the other girls, and her mother soon withdrew her.

The Eucharist was a focus of Teresa's life from an early age. At the age of six, she told her parents that she wanted to receive Holy Communion, later writing, "I was inflamed with desires to receive Our Lord." When she was finally allowed to receive the Eucharist four years later, she described it as a turning point in her life, saying, "from that first embrace, Jesus did not let me go, but took me to Himself."

As early as when she was ten years old, Teresa was graced to hear interior locutions from both Jesus and the Blessed Virgin, calling her to a life of holiness and life within the Carmelite order. Although she was a pious child, she was strong-willed and had a hot temper; she also struggled with vanity, as her natural beauty attracted the attention of many.

Teresa entered the Sacred Heart College, a secondary boarding school, when she was fifteen, where she was an excellent student. Like many teenagers,

Sunday Closest to July 20—Proper 11

she did not like school, describing it as a jail or a dungeon, even expressing the hope that someone would "burn the school down." However, she did consider it to be good training for entering the convent, and she offered the pain of separation from her family to the Lord. It was at this time that Teresa took a private vow of chastity, offering herself to the Lord and committing herself to a life of deep prayer.

Influenced by Thérèse of Lisieux, whose autobiography she read when she was fourteen, Teresa desired to enter the local Carmelite convent at the age of fifteen, and made a vow of virginity on the feast of the Immaculate Conception.

In her last year of school, Teresa began to experience spiritual darkness, doubting her vocation, and even, at times, doubting the existence of God. She was helped through this period by reading the works of Saint John of the Cross, and she came to understand that through the spiritual aridity, she was being called to a deeper level of prayer. Any remaining doubts she may have had were dispelled when she visited the Carmel in Los Andes with her mother and sister in early January 1919.

In May 1919, she entered the small Carmelite monastery about ninety kilometers from Santiago, and received her habit in October, beginning her novitiate. After entering Carmel, her interior prayer life deepened, and she began an apostolate of letter writing, exhorting friends and family members to greater faith in God and service to others. Most of what we know about Teresa comes from her diary, written under holy obedience, and 164 letters to friends, family members, and religious advisors, all of which demonstrate great spiritual maturity for her age.

The month before her death, she had told her confessor that the Lord revealed to her that she would die young, a fate that she accepted with serenity. During Holy Week 1920, Teresa contracted typhus. The course of her final illness was short: on Good Friday, the mother superior noticed that Teresa's cheeks were flushed and called for a doctor. Teresa revealed that she had been feeling sick for about a month, but had hidden her symptoms, accepting her illness as a penance. Her condition continued to deteriorate and by Monday she was slipping in and out of consciousness. She was given Extreme Unction and was allowed, during a period of lucidity, to make her religious vows, which she took with great joy. She died the following Monday, as she was receiving final absolution.

The feast day of Saint Teresa of the Andes in the Roman Catholic Church is April 12; the Order of the Discalced Carmelites also celebrates her on July 13.

This prayer was taken from the diary and letters of Teresa of Los Andes. The illustration is based on a photograph taken in 1919.

Sunday Closest to July 20—Proper 11

JANANI LUWUM

Archbishop (ca. 1922–1977)

We know that all things work together for good for those who love God, who are called according to his purpose.

—Romans 8:28

✢ Friends, let us bring it before the Lord.

O God gives us gifts, and asks us to give back a little of what he gave to us, so that God can use it to enlarge his kingdom and help the needy.

✤ Let us throw down our weapons of resentment and pride and be open with each other.

• I have no weapon but the Bible.

✤ After realizing that my sins were forgiven and the implications of Jesus's death and resurrection, I was overwhelmed by a sense of joy and peace.

• When I was "born again," Christ became the controller of my life.

✤ The Church must help us transfer Christ from our heads into our hearts.

• Even now I am still growing in him.

✤ As Jesus shed his blood for his people, if it is God's will, I do the same.

• I am prepared to die in the army of Jesus.

✤ I live as though there will be no tomorrow. While the opportunity is there, I preach the gospel with all my might.

O I surrender myself to the church.

✢ Do not be afraid. I see the hand of the Lord in this. Bring everything into the light.

O God, the protector of all who trust in you, without whom nothing is strong, nothing is holy: Increase and multiply upon us your mercy; that, with you as our ruler and guide, we may so pass through things temporal, that we lose not the things eternal; through Jesus Christ our Lord, who lives and reigns with you and the Holy Spirit, one God, for ever and ever. *Amen.*

In Janani Luwum, the archbishop of Uganda, Rwanda, Burundi, and Boga-Zaïre, we see a life surrendered to God, proclaiming to the world that the voice of Christ cannot be silenced.

Janani Luwum was born in 1922 in a grass-thatched mud hut in the village of Mucwini in northern Uganda, near the Sudanese border. His father Eliya was an early convert to Christianity and taught at the local church. As a young boy, Janani herded his family's sheep, goats, and cattle on the savanna of East Acholi. He was a popular boy and a skilled hunter, dancer, and musician. Because of his family's limited means, Janani did not begin primary school until the age of ten, however he was an apt student and quickly excelled.

Janani then attended a teacher-training college, where he graduated at the top of his class. Although he had been raised and taught by Christians, Janani did not consider himself a Christian. When an East African revival group visited his village in 1948, Janani's heart was opened to Christ's message of redemption. "Today I have become a leader in Christ's army. I am prepared to die in the army of Jesus," he proclaimed.

The following year, Janani enrolled in the Buwalasi Theological College; he was ordained to the diaconate in 1953, and into the priesthood in 1956. Following his ordination, he studied in England at St. Augustine's College, and later at the London Divinity College. At the conclusion of these studies, Janani returned to Uganda, where he became the principal of the Buwalasi school and served as the provincial secretary. In 1969 he was consecrated as the bishop of the diocese of Northern Uganda; five years later, in 1974, he was elected as the archbishop of Uganda, Rwanda, Burundi, and Boga-Zaïre.

As archbishop, Janani established community development projects to improve conditions for the poor, and empowered the clergy to speak out against violence and injustice. Janani warned Ugandans that "the Church should not conform to the powers of darkness," and courageously confronted the new political administration of Ugandan President Idi Amin, for the brutal regime's growing number of human rights violations.

Janani strove to imitate Christ in his life; his death also bore striking similarities to Christ's Passion.

On February 16, 1977, President Amin summoned Janani, six bishops, and two Christian cabinet ministers to a governmental building in Kampala, where they were accused of treason. A sham trial was held in front of a gathering of soldiers and government officials. When Idi Amin asked the soldiers what Janani's fate should be, they cried out, "Kill him! Kill him!" The other bishops were released, but Janani and the cabinet ministers were taken away by security forces. Janani was stripped of his clothing and brutally beaten. He was executed as he was praying for his tormentors; many believe that Amin himself fired the fatal shot.

The following day, the Amin government announced that Janani had died in a car crash along with two other cabinet ministers. Rather than releasing his body to his grieving widow, the government sealed it in a coffin and transported it to the distant village of Mucwini, his birthplace, where he was buried in a makeshift grave, guarded by the soldiers. When the soldiers left the casket unattended, Janani's nephew and others opened the coffin and discovered a bullet exit wound in the back of his neck; his genital area had been beaten and bandaged. Janani was survived by his wife Mary and nine children.

Janani Luwum was one of the most influential leaders of the modern Church in Africa. He is commemorated in the Anglican Communion on February 17.

His statue is included as one of the ten twentieth-century martyrs on the Great West Door of Westminster Abbey in London.

This prayer was taken from the words of Janani Luwum, as quoted by his personal secretary, Margaret Ford in her biography, *Even Unto Death*. The illustration is based on a photograph of Janani preaching, taken in the mid-1970s, and a drawing by the artist Kwizera.

GREGORY THE GREAT

Monastic, Pope (540–604)

Who will separate us from the love of Christ? Will hardship, or distress, or persecution, or famine, or nakedness, or peril, or sword?

—Romans 8:35

✠ O Lord Jesus, good Shepherd, preserve the just, pardon sinners, have mercy on all the faithful, and be well-disposed to me, a wretched and unworthy sinner.

O Learn the heart of God in the words of God, that your soul may be kindled.

✠ Holy Scripture is placed before the eyes of our mind like a mirror, so that we may view our inner face therein.

• The sacred Scriptures grow with the one who reads them.

✠ We ascend to the heights of contemplation by the steps of action.

• When we attend to the needs of those in want, we give them what is theirs, not ours.

✠ You cannot acquire the gift of peace if by your anger you destroy the peace of the Lord.

• The only true riches are those that make us rich in virtue.

✠ Where love exists, it works great things. But when it ceases to act, it ceases to exist.

• The proof of love is in the works. Where love exists, it does great things.

✠ Whatever you understand of what you hear, you must hasten to put into practice.

✠ The greatness of contemplation can be given to none but those who love.

Let your continual mercy, O Lord, cleanse and defend your Church; and, because it cannot continue in safety without your help, protect and govern it always by your goodness; through Jesus Christ our Lord, who lives and reigns with you and the Holy Spirit, one God, for ever and ever. *Amen.*

*G*regory the Great is remembered for his kindness and charity to the poor as well as for his prolific and significant writing.

Gregory was born in Rome in 540, the son of a wealthy and influential Christian family. His great-great grandfather was Pope Felix III (before priests took vows of celibacy), his father was a Roman senator and prefect of Rome, and his mother and aunt are both saints. He received an excellent education in Latin and Greek as well as in Roman law.

In about 573, Gregory entered public service as the administrative prefect of Rome. It was about that time that Gregory's father died, leaving his numerous properties to Gregory, who sold them, giving a generous portion of the proceeds to the poor, founding six monasteries in Sicily, and transforming his family estate in Rome into a monastery dedicated to Saint Andrew. In 574, Gregory resigned his prefecture and joined the monastery as a monk. Though he had been raised in a Christian household, it was not until he "sought the safe haven of the monastery" that he truly turned away from the secular life. At St. Andrew's, he delighted in contemplative prayer and biblical study, though rigorous asceticism led to chronic health problems.

In 579, Pope Pelagius II ordained Gregory to the diaconate and sent him to Constantinople, where he had both civic and religious responsibilities. In Constantinople, Gregory served with distinction, but was confronted with the tension between the active and contemplative life. It was there that, amid his many responsibilities, he began his massive commentary, *Morals on the Book of Job.* He was recalled to Rome in 585, returning to St. Andrew's, where he served for five years as abbot.

Upon the death of Pelagius II from plague, in 590, the cardinals unanimously elected the reluctant Gregory to be his successor. Gregory, who wished to remain a monk, later wrote to his friend Leander, a Spanish bishop, "weeping, I remember that I have lost the peaceful shore of my retreat." Yet as a "servant of God," he dutifully fulfilled his new responsibilities.

Gregory, who would serve as pontiff until his death in 604, turned out to be one of the most influential popes (one of only three who are called "the Great"). One of his first acts was ordering that produce grown on church-owned lands be sent to Rome for distribution among those suffering from famine. Gregory was known for treating the poor with great charity; at each meal, during his pontificate, he invited a dozen poor people to dine with him; he also required that his clergy care for poor people in the streets.

Gregory put a high priority on mission work, sending Saint Augustine (of Canterbury, not Hippo) to England to support the growth of the church in the British Isles. In addition to his prolific writing Gregory is revered for his theological and spiritual insight. Some have called him the first medieval spiritual author, bridging the gap between the patristic writers of the early Church and the monastic writers of the Middle Ages.

Gregory is often credited with establishing plainsong chant, commonly known as Gregorian Chant, the oldest form of music that is preserved in its original form, though this is probably a legend invented by proponents of unifying liturgical music to bind together worshipers from diverse backgrounds. The thought was that if the chant melodies were attributed to Gregory, they would be more widely received and accepted.

Among his most notable works are his *Dialogues,* his writings on *Pastoral Care,* and his interpretation of the Book of Job. He also wrote *Homilies on Ezekiel,* a *Commentary on 1 Kings,* and *Forty Gospel Homilies.* Upon his death in 604, the people of Rome demanded that he be proclaimed a saint, crying *"Santo subito!"*

Gregory the Great is celebrated March 12 in the Anglican Communion, the Eastern Orthodox Church, and the Lutheran Church, and on September 3 in the Roman Catholic Church.

The prayer for Saint Gregory is taken from his prolific writings. The illustration is from a twelfth-century copy of the *Dialogues*.

JONATHAN MYRICK DANIELS

Seminarian, Martyr (1939–1965)

After these things the word of the Lord came to Abram in a vision, "Do not be afraid, Abram, I am your shield; your reward shall be very great."

—*Genesis 15:1*

☦ My dear friends, I wish you the joy of a purposeful life.

O I wish you new worlds and the vision to see them.

⁜ We who call ourselves Christians must learn better the Way of the Cross.

• The Way of the Cross is the road of life.

⁜ Though I cannot guess precisely where I am being driven, I am flying with the mightiest Wind at my back.

• Gradually, surely, mysteriously, wonderfully, my faith is growing.

⁜ I am a servant of Christ, the possibility of death cannot be a deciding factor for me.

• The risk is great—but so is the joy.

⁜ The revolution to which I am committed is the way of the Cross.

• The ongoing sacrifice of the Cross is the only triumph of significant value.

⁜ The gospel is a matter of living and dying and living anew.

O We must pray for strength to carry a cross.

☦ In Him Whose Name is above all names, we are indelibly, unspeakably *one*.

Grant to us, Lord, we pray, the spirit to think and do always those
things that are right, that we, who cannot exist without you, may by
you be enabled to live according to your will; through Jesus Christ our
Lord, who lives and reigns with you and the Holy Spirit, one God, for
ever and ever. *Amen.*

*B*orn in 1939 in Keene, New Hampshire, Jonathan Myrick Daniels
was the son of a prominent physician and his wife. He was strongly
influenced by his father's humanitarian efforts, serving as a physician during
World War II. As a child, Jonathan attended religious summer camps and
attended church with his family. He loved writing and wrote a prophetic short
story, while in high school, about an urban priest who was shot while protecting
a young woman.

Jonathan attended the Virginia Military Institute where he graduated
with honors and was elected class valedictorian. His father's death in 1959
led Jonathan to question his faith and religious calling; he abandoned his
intention to become a priest, pursuing graduate studies in English at Harvard
University, instead. While at Harvard, still grieving his father's death and
facing his family's financial struggles, Jonathan suffered a major depressive
episode. That spring, on Easter Sunday 1962, Jonathan underwent a profound
religious experience and returned to the church; he decided to leave Harvard
and seek Holy Orders.

In fall 1962, Jonathan enrolled at the Episcopal Theological Seminary in
Cambridge, Massachusetts. In the fall of his second year at seminary, he par-
ticipated in local demonstrations against racism and social injustice, and joined
the NAACP. That summer, for his seminary field placement, he worked with

poor and disadvantaged youth in Providence, Rhode Island, an experience that he said helped him grow "experientially, ethically, and spiritually."

Jonathan saw the television coverage of Alabama state troopers violently attacking the peaceful protesters marching from Selma to Montgomery, Alabama. He heard the call of Dr. Martin Luther King Jr. calling for White clergy from the northern United States to come to Selma to join the march. While Jonathan was singing the Magnificat during Evening Prayer, he heard the words, "He hath put down the mighty from their seat, and hath exalted the humble and meek" as a personal call to go to Selma.

Jonathan and ten other students from the seminary went to Selma to join the march. The march was halted when the leaders were presented with a court order to stop. Later, a federal judge lifted the ban, allowing Jonathan and thousands of others to make the four-day march to Montgomery. He continued working for social justice until May, when he returned to the seminary for his exams. He returned to Alabama that summer, continuing to work for voting rights.

After being sprayed with tear gas at a voter-registration rally in Camden, Alabama, Jonathan began to experience a change of heart toward the White law enforcement officers charged with breaking up the protests. "I saw that the men who came at me were themselves, not free . . .I began to discover a new freedom in the Cross . . .freedom to love the enemy. And in that freedom, to will and to try to set him free."

Jonathan returned to the seminary in May to complete his coursework. His family urged him to stay home, but he returned to Alabama in July. In August, he was arrested at a protest and held at a local jail. When the protesters were released six days later, Jonathan and three others went to a nearby store to buy soft drinks. They were met in the doorway of the store by Tom Coleman who aimed a shotgun at one of the young Black women in the group. Jonathan pushed her aside, taking the full force of the blast at close range and died instantly; he was twenty-six years old.

Jonathan is honored in the martyrs' chapel in Canterbury Cathedral in England and with a bust at the entrance to the Washington National Cathedral. He is commemorated by the Episcopal Church on August 14 and by the Anglican Church of North America on August 21.

This prayer is taken from Jonathan's letters, sermons, and his valedictory address to the Virginia Military Institute Class of 1961. The illustration is based on an icon written by Mark Friesland.

THOMAS À KEMPIS

Monastic, Priest, Theologian, Mystic

(1380–1471)

For the gifts and the calling of God are irrevocable.

—*Romans 11:29*

✠ Enlighten me, blessed Jesus, with the brightness of Your inner light, and cast away all darkness that lives in my heart.

O Send forth Your light and Your truth to shine on the earth, for I am like earth, empty and formless until You illumine me. Pour out Your grace from above. Shower my heart with heavenly dew.

✠ Whoever wishes to understand the words of Christ must try to pattern their whole life on that of Christ.

• If you seek Jesus in all things, you will surely find Him.

✠ Visit me often, and teach me Your holy discipline so that, healed and purified within, I may be fit to love, strong to suffer, and firm to persevere.

• The more you die to yourself, the more you begin to live in God.

✠ There is no salvation of soul nor hope of everlasting life but in the cross.

• Cling, therefore, to Jesus in life and death.

✠ Trust yourself to the glory of Him Who alone can help you when all others fail.

• When Jesus is present, all is well and nothing seems difficult.

O Once you have given yourself completely to God, not pursuing your own will and desires but instead settling yourself entirely on Him, you will find yourself united and at peace.

✠ Grant most merciful Jesus, that Your grace may be with me, and work with me, and remain with me to the very end.

Almighty God, you have given your only Son to be for us a sacrifice for sin, and also an example of godly life: Give us grace to receive thankfully the fruits of his redeeming work, and to follow daily in the blessed steps of his most holy life; through Jesus Christ your Son our Lord, who lives and reigns with you and the Holy Spirit, one God, now and for ever. *Amen.*

It is believed that *The Imitation of Christ,* by Thomas à Kempis, has influenced more Christians than any book other than the Bible; his words inspire us still.

Thomas Hemerkin, born in 1380 in Kempen, near Düsseldorf, Germany, is better known today by the name Thomas à Kempis, after his birthplace. His father was a blacksmith (hence the surname Hemerkin, or "little hammer") and his mother was a schoolmistress, both pious Christians. From his boyhood, Thomas held a deep devotion to the Virgin Mary and offered daily devotions to her.

When Thomas was twelve, he left home to join his twin brother Johannes at the cathedral school in Deventer, Netherlands, run by the Brethren of the Common Life, a lay religious community devoted to education and the care of the poor. There he studied under the theologian Florens Radewijns, who recognized Thomas as a diligent youth of unusual piety and provided for the boy's tuition, arranging for housing with a "noble and devout lady." Thomas remained at the school in Deventer until 1399.

Around 1408 Thomas, sensing a vocational calling, entered the Augustinian Congregation of Windesheim, a group of canons regular who lived in community with his brother serving as their prior. Canons regular live under ecclesiastical rule and are bound by religious vows; their calling combines elements of monastic devotional life with the pastoral ministry of priests. At the monastery of Mount St. Agnes, in the city of Zwolle, Thomas was ordained a priest in 1413, was made subprior of the monastery in 1429, and served as the novice master. Thomas remained with the community for more than seventy-one years.

One night, Thomas had a dream in which he was teaching his novices and the Virgin Mary appeared standing on a cloud coming down from heaven. She gently embraced each student and kissed them with maternal love, but when she finally got to Thomas, she said, "Why have your prayers vanished? Has your love for me grown cold? You are unworthy of my embrace, since you have neglected such an easy thing as to offer a daily greeting to your beloved." After her well-deserved admonition, she disappeared and Thomas woke from his dream and never again allowed a day to pass without offering homage to the Virgin.

In his capacity as novice master, Thomas wrote four booklets that were compiled into a single volume, now known as *The Imitation of Christ,* written between about 1420 and 1427. In the first treatise, he wrote, "We must imitate Christ's life and his ways if we are to be truly enlightened and set free from the darkness of our own hearts." Thomas was a prolific author across many genres, including hagiographies, scriptural commentaries, biographies of the leaders of the Brotherhood of Common Life, works of spiritual instruction, homilies, prayers, and letters; his collected works comprise eight volumes.

Thomas was a skilled and devoted copyist of manuscripts, transcribing at least four copies of the entire Bible, the complete works of Bernard of Clairvaux, and works by Augustine and other early church fathers.

Thomas died peacefully near Zolle in 1471, at the age of ninety-two. Such diverse thinkers as Ignatius of Loyola, John Wesley, Henry VIII, Oscar Wilde, and Thérèse of Lisieux have all thought *The Imitation of Christ* was the most important book for a Christian to own after the Bible. Although he is commemorated in the Anglican Communion and Lutheran Church, he is beatified, but not canonized, in the Roman Catholic Church. According to legend, when Thomas's body was exhumed, scratch marks were found on the inside of his coffin, which were believed to indicate he didn't die in a state of perfect grace, considered a disqualifying factor for sainthood.

Thomas à Kempis is commemorated on July 24 in the Anglican Communion and the Lutheran Church.

This prayer was taken from *The Imitation of Christ*. The illustration is based on a copperplate engraving after Esme de Boulonois, 1682.

HENRY BUDD

SAKACHUWESCUM

Priest and Missionary (ca. 1812–1875)

Listen to me, my people, and give heed to me, my nation; for a teaching will go out from me, and my justice for a light to the peoples.

—Isaiah 51:4

✝ O, that the Sun of righteousness would sanctify our hearts to enable us this day to worship Him in Spirit and in truth.

O The more I meditate on the sovereign mercy and love of our Heavenly Father, the more I feel I cannot do enough for Him.

⳨ Enter the sacred walls with hearts prepared by the Spirit of God, to receive the seed of the Word.

• By His Spirit make fit and prepare our hearts.

⳨ Oh, that we may be enabled to worship Him in spirit and in truth, that He may fill us with ever blessed influences of his Holy Spirit.

• Trust in the assisting grace of God.

⳨ May the Lord whose Spirit alone can illuminate our dark minds, bless the Word to each of our hearts.

• Feast from the treasury of God's Holy Word.

⳨ Lord make us ready and prepare us for dedicating ourselves to your Service, soul, body, and Spirit.

• Give ourselves afresh to the service of God.

⳨ May the Lord cause his holy Word to bring forth in us the fruit of good living to the praise and glory of his holy Name.

O May we have grace to turn again and again to Him who has power in his hands and compassion in his heart to bind up our broken Spirit.

✝ May a gracious God hear and answer our prayers, and mercifully by His grace enable us to bring forth fruit to His glory.

Grant, O merciful God, that your Church, being gathered together in unity by your Holy Spirit, may show forth your power among all peoples, to the glory of your Name; through Jesus Christ our Lord, who lives and reigns with you and the Holy Spirit, one God, for ever and ever. *Amen.*

*H*enry Budd, the first Indigenous American to be ordained an Anglican priest, brought the Gospel of Jesus to the Cree Nation. Sakachuwescum, whose name means "Going Up the Hill," was a member of the Cree Métis people, born circa 1812 in Norway House, Canada, a fur-trading post on the Hudson Bay. He was raised by his mother, as his father died either before he was born or early during his infancy. In 1820, his mother placed him with the Reverend John West, the first chaplain of the Hudson's Bay Company (HBC), for education in the Christian faith. At his baptism, Sakachuwescum was given the name "Henry Budd," after a vicar with whom John West had worked in England and who provided support for his namesake with gifts of money and books.

John West brought Henry to the Red River settlement where he was enrolled in the mission school. In addition to instruction in English, mathematics, and spiritual matters, each pupil was allotted a garden plot and was "trained in industry upon the soil." Henry was a superior student, noted for his "quickness of apprehension"; by 1823 he spoke English fluently.

In 1829, his schooling complete, Henry moved to the "Lower Church" area along the Red River, where he lived with his mother, his brother's widow, and her three children. After receiving a land grant from the HBC in 1831, Henry supported his family through farming, and by working as a "voyageur" for HBC from 1832 to 1835, translating between English and the Cree language.

In 1836, Henry married Betsy Work, an Irish-Cree woman with whom he had at least eight children. Henry became a teacher and schoolmaster with the Church Missionary Society in 1837, taking charge of a mission school. Three years later he established a new Anglican mission headquarters in The Pas, Manitoba, where he was known as a skilled translator, passionate pastor, fruitful evangelist, and an excellent administrator.

By 1842, Henry had attracted thirty-one pupils to his mission school. In addition, Sunday services attracted about twenty adults weekly. Henry's work as a catechist and proselytizer was bearing fruit: in 1844 there were ninety-two candidates for baptism, and then 212 in 1845, growing to a peak of 663 in 1854.

Because of Henry's skill and passion as an orator he was recommended for ordination and was trained under the supervision of the local bishop. In 1850, at the age of thirty-eight, he was ordained as a deacon and three years later was ordained a priest, making him the first Indigenous person to be ordained an Anglican priest in North America. Following his ordination, Henry was given a new mission in Saskatchewan, where he taught and served for fifteen years.

Working with the Reverend James Hunter, Henry undertook a translation of the Bible into the Cree language; by 1853, he had translated all 150 psalms. Eventually, he translated the Bible and the *Book of Common Prayer*. As a result of his educational outreach, most of the older Cree living near the mission could read and write in the Cree syllabic system by 1854, making it possible for them to read the Bible in their homes. By necessity, his responsibilities also included building the churches and schoolhouses.

In 1857 Henry and his family moved to an even more remote mission. Here he experienced great personal tragedy followed by periods of depression. A scarlet fever epidemic in 1864 took the lives of his wife, eldest son, and a teenage daughter; a second son also died that summer. Henry sent four other children to Red Rock, but kept his nine-year-old son with him. In 1874, he suffered the loss of his youngest son. Henry Budd died of influenza in 1875 at the age of sixty-one.

Sunday Closest to August 24—Proper 16

Henry Budd is commemorated by the Anglican Church of Canada and the Anglican Church of North America on April 2.

This prayer is taken from *The Diary of the Reverend Henry Budd.* The drawing is based on an illustration by Ben Lansing and an undated photograph.

BERNARD OF CLAIRVAUX

Abbot, Theologian, Mystic (1090–1153)

Prove me, O Lord, and try me; test my heart and mind. For your steadfast love is before my eyes, and I walk in faithfulness to you.

—*Psalms 26:2–3*

✠ The reason for loving God is God Himself.

○ Those who praise God because he is Goodness itself, are children doing homage to their father.

☩ Love seeks no cause beyond itself and no fruit; it is its own fruit, its own enjoyment.

• I love in order that I may love.

☩ I love God not because he meets my needs; but because I have tasted and I know how sweet the Lord is.

• The law of love is good and sweet.

☩ Jesus to me is honey in the mouth, music in the ear, a song in the heart.

• What we love we shall grow to resemble.

☩ Love flows back into its source, it always draws from it the power to flow forth continuously.

• The measure of love is to love without measure.

☩ Love is the law of the Lord, which holds and unites the Trinity in unity in the bonds of peace.

○ The God of peace pacifies all things.

✠ God will become visible as God's image is reborn in you.

Lord of all power and might, the author and giver of all good things: Graft in our hearts the love of your Name; increase in us true religion; nourish us with all goodness; and bring forth in us the fruit of good works; through Jesus Christ our Lord, who lives and reigns with you and the Holy Spirit, one God for ever and ever. *Amen.*

Saint Bernard of Clairvaux, the "honey-tongued Doctor of the Church," who guided Dante through Paradise in the *Divine Comedy,* guides us in love toward union with God.

Bernard was born in a castle near Dijon, France, in 1090, to a knight and his wife of Burgundian nobility. His mother dedicated him to God at birth and instilled in him a lifelong devotion to Mary. As a youth Bernard studied at a nearby school staffed by canons regular where he excelled in Latin, literature, and rhetoric. After his mother's death, when Bernard was seventeen, he experienced a period of depression, which was a turning point in his "long path to complete conversion."

Bernard's charism for leadership was apparent from an early age. In 1112, at the age of twenty-two, he persuaded four of his brothers and twenty-six other kinsmen and Burgundian noblemen to join him in entering the newly formed monastery at Citeaux, from which the Cistercian Order would get its name. Three years later, his abbot sent Bernard and twelve other monks to form a new monastery in Champagne, where Bernard served as abbot; he named the spot Clairvaux, or "clear valley." The new monastery thrived, attracting many to monastic life. At the time of Bernard's death, he and his monks had established more than 150 new Cistercian monasteries.

At the urging of his prior, Bernard wrote *The Steps of Humility and Pride* in 1124. This was followed by his *Letter on Love,* which is also included in his later treatise *On Loving God.* He was a prolific and eloquent letter writer—it is said that he never left a letter unanswered—corresponding with abbots, bishops, popes, and kings. At the Council of Troyes in 1128, where Bernard served as secretary, he wrote the Rule for the Knights Templar, establishing a new standard for Christian nobility.

The years between 1130 and 1150 marked the most active and influential period of Bernard's life. Because of his growing influence, Bernard was instrumental in helping the Roman Church resolve the papal schism that emerged after the death of Pope Honorius II in 1130, advocating that the true successor was Innocent II. He publicly denounced Peter Abelard for heretical writings, and the two were set to debate in 1141 before a council of bishops, but after hearing Bernard's opening statement, Abelard withdrew from the debate and submitted to discipline. At the urging of Pope Eugenius III and King Louis VII of France, Bernard preached throughout France and Germany, exhorting Christians to join the Second Crusade (1146–50), which ended in failure and defeat at Damascus.

In addition to his writings and wise council, Bernard was widely regarded as a faith healer and worker of miracles during his lifetime. Once, when his monastery was beset with flies, Bernard excommunicated the flies; the following morning, not a single fly was found alive. Such was his reputation that wherever he traveled, the sick and injured lined the roads, seeking his healing. Crowds surrounded his lodging places in such numbers that an archdeacon traveling with him joked that that the biggest miracle was the fact that Bernard survived the crowds.

Bernard claimed that his extensive knowledge of Holy Scripture came from meditating and praying in the woods and fields, saying, "I have no other masters than the beeches and the oaks." The final years of his life were spent writing his *Sermons on the Song of Songs,* in which Bernard uses mystical and allegorical exegesis to liken the love between a bridegroom and bride to the union of the soul with God. In these eighty-six sermons, Bernard covered only up to the first verse of the third chapter of the text.

Sunday Closest to August 31—Proper 17

Throughout his life, Bernard suffered from poor health, including migraines, gastritis, and anemia, exacerbated by his lifelong ascetic discipline of fasting, sleep deprivation, and other bodily mortifications. Bernard died at Clairvaux in 1153.

Bernard of Clairvaux is celebrated throughout the Western church on August 20.

> This prayer is taken from Bernard's *Sermons on the Song of Songs,* his treatise *On Loving God,* and his letters. The illustration was inspired by a depiction of Bernard and his pupils from a thirteenth-century English manuscript.

EDITH STEIN

TERESA BENEDICTA OF THE CROSS

Monastic and Martyr (1891–1942)

Let Israel be glad in its Maker; let the children of Zion rejoice in their King.

—Psalms 149:2

✝ O Lord, full of love, bend your ear to my quiet words and deeply fill my heart with peace.

O Who are you, sweet light, that fills me and illumines the darkness of my heart?

✤ The work of salvation takes place in the heart's quiet dialogue with God.

• Authentic prayer is the fruit of union with Christ.

✤ God wants to be found by those who seek him with their whole hearts.

• All those who seek truth, seek God.

✤ Whoever loves with Christ's love will want people for God and not for himself.

• The love of Christ never withdraws in the face of hatred.

✤ The innermost essence of love is self-offering. The entryway to all things is the Cross.

• Surrender without reservation to the Lord who has called us.

✤ To suffer with Christ is to cooperate with him in his work of salvation.

O The heart of Jesus, which was pierced, is the source of life.

✝ We must go to the world to carry the divine life into it.

Grant us, O Lord, to trust in you with all our hearts; for, as you always resist the proud who confide in their own strength, so you never forsake those who make their boast of your mercy; through Jesus Christ our Lord, who lives and reigns with you and the Holy Spirit, one God, now and for ever. *Amen.*

*E*dith Stein had a deep love for the truth and pursued it from the heights of philosophical discourse to the depths of contemplative silence; from her Jewish roots through the Carmel to Auschwitz.

Edith Stein, born on Yom Kippur in 1891, was the youngest of eleven children born to an observant Jewish family in Breslau, Germany. Edith was a brilliant student and an avid reader; to her classmates she was a good-natured and empathetic friend. As a young teenager, Edith began to turn away from the God of her Jewish faith and stopped praying.

In 1911 Edith entered university to study with the philosopher Edmund Husserl, eventually earning her doctoral degree *summa cum laude* for her dissertation, "The Problem of Empathy." There she encountered Christianity through students and faculty, including Adolf Reinach, who was killed in World War I in 1917. When Edith visited his grieving widow, she witnessed the power of the cross, describing this visit as "the moment when my unbelief collapsed and Christ began to shine His light on me."

Edith continued exploring Christianity through reading the Bible and the spiritual exercises of Saint Ignatius of Loyola. In 1921, while visiting friends who were Lutherans, Edith read the autobiography of Saint Teresa of Ávila. When she finished the book, she declared to herself, "This is the truth," understanding that God is not a God of knowledge, but a God of love.

Edith was baptized on New Year's Day 1922. Reflecting on her spiritual journey, she would write, "I had given up practicing my Jewish religion when I was a 14-year-old girl and did not begin to feel Jewish again until I had returned to God," belonging to Christ both by blood and by spirit. She was later confirmed by the bishop of Speyer on the Feast of the Purification of the Blessed Virgin Mary. At this time, Edith wanted to become a Discalced Carmelite nun, but her spiritual director advised her to wait.

From 1923 through 1931, Edith taught at a teachers' training school at St. Magdalen's Convent in Cologne, Germany. During this time, she translated works of John Henry Newman and Thomas Aquinas into German, a practice of "scholarship in service to God." In 1933, she wrote to Pope Pius XI urging him to write an encyclical in defense of the Jewish people, but her request, possibly mishandled, went unanswered.

Edith entered the Discalced Carmelite monastery in Cologne in the fall of 1933, where she took the religious name of Teresa Benedicta of the Cross. She made her final profession in 1938, taking on the words of Saint John of the Cross: "Henceforth my only vocation is to love." It was at the Cologne Carmel that Edith wrote her magnum opus, *Finite and Eternal Being,* a synthesis of the philosophies of Husserl, Thomas Aquinas, and John Duns Scotus.

In the wake of the Nazi violence of *Kristallnacht,* November 9, 1938, it became undeniably clear to Edith that her remaining at the Cologne Carmel would put the safety of her sisters in jeopardy. Two months later, in January 1939, she was smuggled across the border into the Netherlands where she took refuge in the Carmel in Echt. From Echt, she wrote her memoir, *The Life of a Jewish Family,* as a witness to her familial heritage. "I accept the death God has prepared for me in complete submission and with joy as being his most holy will for me."

On August 2, 1942, Edith and her sister Rosa, who had also converted and become a Carmelite, were arrested by the Gestapo while they were worshiping in the convent chapel. In retaliation for a letter from the Dutch Catholic bishops denouncing the Nazis' treatment of Jews, an order was issued for the arrest of Catholics of Jewish descent. Edith and Rosa were transported to a transit camp before arriving at Auschwitz on August 7. It is believed that Edith and her sister were gassed on August 9, 1942.

The feast day for Saint Edith Stein is celebrated in the Roman Catholic Church on August 9.

This prayer is taken from the collected works of Edith Stein. The illustration is based on a passport photo taken around 1938.

GERTRUDE THE GREAT

Monastic, Mystic, Theologian (1256–1302)

If we live, we live to the Lord, and if we die, we die to the Lord; so then, whether we live or whether we die, we are the Lord's.

—Romans 14:8

✠ Holy Trinity, one God: grant that my heart may fear you, cherish you, and follow you because you are my true love.

O O wondrous Wisdom of God, make me pleasing to you in humility of spirit, in ready obedience, and in the blessed consummation of your cherishing love.

✠ Jesus, good shepherd, make me hear and acknowledge your voice apart from everything that keeps me from you.

• Let me become one heart and soul with Jesus.

✠ Send your Holy Spirit straightaway and create in me a new heart and a new spirit.

• Enlighten me to recognize you; set me on fire to love you.

✠ Renew me in yourself and make me holy, that you may transport yourself into my soul.

• Take possession of me that I may truly yearn for you.

✠ I place my life in the guardianship of your Holy Spirit so that I may keep your commandments at all times.

• What would be most pleasing to you at this moment, O Lord?

✠ Growing strong in you, I may again become green and, sanctified in truth, again begin to flower.

O You are the exhilaration of my spirit, the praise of my heart and mouth, my Jesus: I will follow you wherever you go.

✠ Teach me how I may fear you, show me how I may cherish you, instruct me how I may follow you. *Amen.*

O God, because without you we are not able to please you, mercifully grant that your Holy Spirit may in all things direct and rule our hearts; through Jesus Christ our Lord, who lives and reigns with you and the Holy Spirit, one God, now and for ever. *Amen.*

*G*ertrude's great devotion and spiritual union with the Lord, along with the simple, yet profound grace of her writing, inspire us to deepen our own devotion to Jesus Christ.

Gertrude the Great (also called Gertrude of Helfta) was born on the Feast of the Epiphany in 1256. Nothing is known of her parents or place of birth—there is no mention of her family name in the monastery records—but she entered the great Benedictine monastery at Helfta for education and formation in 1261, when she was only five years old, and stayed there for the rest of her life. Gertrude's writings hint that she may have been an orphan, but at the abbey, she was placed under the care and tutelage of Mechthild of Hackeborn who became her spiritual mother.

Young Gertrude flourished at the abbey; she was an exceptional student with a passion for learning, who quickly mastered the traditional liberal arts: grammar, logic, rhetoric, astronomy, arithmetic, geometry, and music. By her own later admission, she prided herself on her academic accomplishments, especially her scholarship in Latin. Though she busied herself with prayer and study throughout her youth, it was during Advent 1280 that Gertrude awakened to her own pridefulness and turned to God in humility, praying for a conversion of her heart.

In late January 1281, when Gertrude was twenty-five, she had a vision in which a young man took her by the hand, and with gentle sweetness guided her out of a thorny entanglement that was surrounding her soul. By the wounds on his hands, the "young man" was revealed to her to be "the One who saved us with his Blood on the Cross: Jesus." This experience, which Gertrude referred to as "the day of my salvation," was a turning point in her life, beginning her transformation from a grammarian and secular scholar to a theologian. She put aside the works of the secular writers whom she had formerly enjoyed and focused her great intellect on Holy Scripture and the writings of Saint Augustine, Saint Gregory the Great, and Bernard of Clairvaux.

The change in her intellectual focus was accompanied by a parallel shift in her monastic observance, from what Gertrude described as "negligence" to a life of intense mystical prayer and zeal for the Gospel. She described this event as effectively dividing her life into two distinct chapters, although her change of heart occurred gradually over time. In one of her most memorable visions, the Christ child exchanged hearts with her, giving her the capacity to love the world through his heart. Gertrude's life and mystical writings were suffused by her love for Christ and her longing for oneness with him, which she describes with vivid and daring imagery, reminiscent of the Song of Solomon, describing her mystical union with Christ.

The major works of Gertrude that survived the destruction of the Helfta monastery in 1525 are the five-volume *Herald of Divine Love,* a distillation of her spiritual experiences and revelations, along with a *vita* compiled by her sisters, and her *Spiritual Exercises,* which Pope Benedict XVI has called "a rare jewel of mystical spiritual literature."

In her later years, Gertrude suffered from poor health, though she was able to continue working as a spiritual director. She died on November 17 in 1301 or 1302, at the age of about forty-six, writing shortly before her death, "O Jesus, bless my passing, so that my spirit, freed from the bonds of the flesh, may immediately find rest in you. Amen."

The feast day for Saint Gertrude in the Roman Catholic Church is November 16; in the Anglican Communion she is commemorated with Mechthild of Hackeborn on November 21.

Sunday Closest to September 14—Proper 19

This prayer was taken from the *Spiritual Exercises* of Gertrude the Great. The illustration is based on an eighteenth-century engraving by Giuseppe Foschi, now part of the Wellcome Collection.

THÉRÈSE OF LISIEUX

Monastic, Doctor of the Church (1873–1897)

For to me, living is Christ and dying is gain. . . . For he has graciously granted you the privilege not only of believing in Christ, but of suffering for him as well.

—*Phil. 1:21, 29*

✠ O My God! Most Blessed Trinity, I desire to *Love* You and make You *Loved*.

O Jesus, may earthly things have no power to disturb the peace of my soul; peace is all I ask of you, except love—love that is as infinite as you are.

✠ When you love God the capacities of your heart are enlarged.

• Love is the vocation which includes all others.

✠ Gracious Jesus, your will is to love, in and through me, all the people you tell me to love!

• O my God, I offer myself to your merciful love.

✠ Miss no single opportunity of making some small sacrifice; doing the smallest thing and doing it all for love.

• To love you here on earth, I have only today.

✠ The only way that leads to Love's furnace is the way of self-surrender.

• My strength lies in prayer and sacrifice; they are invincible weapons.

✠ To You alone, O Jesus, I must cling; and running to Your arms, dear Lord, there let me hide; loving with childlike tenderness.

O No harm can come to me; in whatever happens, I see only the tender hand of Jesus.

✠ Oh, I love Him! My God, I love you!

Grant us, Lord, not to be anxious about earthly things, but to love things heavenly; and even now, while we are placed among things that are passing away, to hold fast to those that shall endure; through Jesus Christ our Lord, who lives and reigns with you and the Holy Spirit, one God, for ever and ever. *Amen.*

Thérèse of Lisieux and her "little way," teach us how to live ordinary lives with extraordinary love.

Thérèse was born in 1873 to devout parents in Alençon, France. Thérèse, the youngest of five surviving children, had a happy early childhood and later wrote that her life was "imprinted with the most tender smiles and caresses." After her mother died from breast cancer when Thérèse was four, her eldest sister Pauline became like a second mother to her. Within a few months of her mother's death, her father moved the family to Lisieux.

Thérèse's time in Lisieux, before entering the Carmel, was difficult for her, and she became withdrawn and melancholy. Initially her older sisters Pauline and Marie tutored the precocious girl, but in 1881, she was enrolled in the local Benedictine Abbey school. The following fall, her sister Pauline left home to enter the Carmelite monastery, causing Thérèse great anguish, and leaving her bereft of maternal affection for a second time. Although Thérèse wanted to enter the monastery, the prioress told her that she was too young.

The winter after Pauline's departure, Thérèse entered a period of intense physical and spiritual suffering that included bouts of fever, hallucinations, insomnia, and nearly constant migraines. Thérèse looked at a statue of the Virgin near her bed and prayed for a cure. As she gazed at the statue, "Mary's face radiated kindness and love" and smiled at Thérèse, who was miraculously cured of her illness. On Christmas Eve 1886, coming home from midnight

Mass, Thérèse experienced what she described as an inner conversion in which she was freed from her selfish childhood desires and her "heart was filled with charity."

When Thérèse was fourteen, she again expressed her desire to enter the Carmelite monastery, but was told that she was still too young. Thérèse then appealed unsuccessfully to the bishop to intercede on her behalf. Her zeal for religious life was so strong that while receiving a papal blessing during a pilgrimage to Rome—even though she had been admonished not to speak to the Holy Father—she tearfully asked that *he* allow her to enter the Carmel. The Pope told her to do as her superiors instructed. Unsatisfied, Thérèse rested her hands on his knees and asked again, to which the Pope replied, "Go. You will enter if God wills it." Then two armed papal guards physically led her away. Just a few months later, however, her wish was granted, and Thérèse entered the Carmel at Lisieux.

In April 1888, Thérèse was received into the monastery and professed her vows in September 1890. By all accounts, her novitiate was unremarkable; the other sisters in her community saw her as a good nun, but not an outstanding one. While her exterior life was unexceptional, a transformation took place in Thérèse's heart; she was graced with the insight of "the little way": doing the smallest actions with great love. Accepting her own insignificance, she relied on God's help in all things, thus her "littleness" and limitations became her great joy, proving her love for others with "every little sacrifice, every glance and word, and the doing of the least actions for love."

The last years of Thérèse's life were marked by a steady decline in her health. On Good Friday 1896, she coughed up blood, a sign, she thought, that she was to share in Christ's suffering and Passion. Her condition worsened and she withdrew from communal activities, entering the convent infirmary in July 1897. During the final stages of her illness, her pain was so intense that she asked to have all poisonous medications removed from her reach, to spare her the temptation of suicide, which she considered a sin. She died on September 30, 1897; her last words were, "Oh, I love Him, my God, I love you."

Sunday Closest to September 21—Proper 20

The feast day for Saint Thérèse of the Child Jesus and of the Holy Face is celebrated in the Roman Catholic Church on October 1.

This prayer is taken from Thérèse's autobiography, *A Story of a Soul* and quotes transcribed by her Sisters. The illustration is based on a photograph taken in the early 1890s.

TERESA OF ÁVILA

Mystic, Poet, Monastic Reformer (1515–1582)

I will open my mouth in a parable; I will utter dark sayings from of old, things that we have heard and known, that our ancestors have told us.

—Psalms 78:2–3

✠ Oh, my Beloved, my greatest good! Our only hope is in trying to understand Your will and losing ourselves in serving You.

O To my God I have surrendered: my Love belongs to me, and I belong to Him.

⚜ Whenever we think of Christ we should recall the love that led Him to bestow on us so many graces and favors; for love calls love in return.

• Love, when mature, cannot exist without action.

⚜ Let's follow Jesus, our pathway and our light.

• Sweet Love, for you, I was born—What do you command of me?

⚜ For the soul abandoned completely to God, the Cross is the tree of life.

• The Cross alone is the way to heaven.

⚜ Leave it all to God and leave your interests in His hands. He knows what is fitting for you.

• Let nothing disturb you, Let nothing frighten you.

⚜ Beg favor from Jesus, who is your light. He will be your defender in times of trouble.

O Whoever has God lacks nothing; God alone suffices.

✠ May God our Beloved be forever blessed and praised. *Amen.*

O God, you declare your almighty power chiefly in showing mercy and pity: Grant us the fullness of your grace, that we, running to obtain your promises, may become partakers of your heavenly treasure; through Jesus Christ our Lord, who lives and reigns with you and the Holy Spirit, one God, for ever and ever. *Amen.*

Teresa of Ávila calls us to prayer and shows us the way, through her daily life wholly oriented to God, and through her writings.

Teresa was born in Ávila, Spain, in 1515 to devout, God-fearing parents. As a child, she loved to read about the lives of the saints with her brother, Rodrigo. Seeking to attain quickly the treasures of heaven, the children decided to become martyrs and set off by foot for "the country of the Moors." Their uncle found the wandering children and returned them to their mother, to her great relief. Thwarted at becoming a martyr, Teresa's play turned to building imaginary hermitages and convents, and pretending to be a hermit or a nun.

After the death of her mother when Teresa was thirteen, she wept before a statue of Mary, imploring the Blessed Virgin to become her new mother. Teresa's devotion to Mary and the rosary would continue throughout her life. However, during Teresa's teenage years, her interests turned to typical adolescent vanities, leading her father to sent her to a convent run by Augustinian nuns, where she began praying regularly. However, "grievous infirmities," including fever, pain, and fainting spells, forced her to return to the care of her relatives.

In 1536, having recovered her health, Teresa entered a Carmelite monastery (without her father's consent), making her profession the following year. There, she developed another serious illness, causing her to return to her family's care. She read Francisco de Osuna's *The Spiritual Alphabet,* which introduced her to new ways of prayer. Teresa's condition worsened; she received last rites, fell into a coma, and appeared to be dead. During the death vigil, however, she gasped for breath. Though paralyzed and bedridden, Teresa asked to be returned to the convent. Gradually, over three years, her health improved and she recovered the ability to walk. For nearly twenty years, Teresa's life in the convent was hidden and unremarkable.

As Teresa approached the age of forty, she began having a flood of mystical experiences. In 1554, she fell prostrate before a statue of the scourged Christ, weeping uncontrollably. Following this, she experienced a stream of visions and locutions exhorting her to a life of deep and purifying prayer. Her frequent raptures and ecstasies produced trancelike states that could last for hours; these visions culminated in 1560 with a transverberation in which her heart was pierced by a flaming arrow of love, an experience both intensely sweet and agonizingly painful. She felt so perfectly united with God, that His will was her only desire.

As her prayer life deepened, Teresa became discontent with the lax practices within her order. In 1562 she requested permission from Pope Pius IV to found a reformed convent; over the next twenty years she would establish some seventeen reformed monasteries, many founded with her friend, confessor, and spiritual advisor, Saint John of the Cross, whom she met in 1567 and invited to join her in reforming the Carmelite order. She persisted in her reforming efforts despite considerable resistance and hostility within the Carmelite order and from civic authorities. Teresa wrote for support to King Philip II who intervened on her behalf, helping the Discalced Carmelites become recognized as a separate province within the order. Teresa died in 1582, twelve years before the Discalced Carmelites gained independence as a distinct order.

Although she had no formal training in theology, Teresa is one of the Church's greatest teachers on the way of prayer. Her autobiography, *The Life of Teresa of Jesus,* written under holy obedience, gives a detailed account of her spiritual journey. In *The Way of Perfection,* she instructs her sisters on living a life of prayer. *The Interior Castle,* her *magnum opus,* which continues her exploration of prayer, is a classic of Christian spiritual writing.

Teresa of Ávila is celebrated throughout the Western Church on October 15. In 1970, she became the first woman to be named a Doctor of the Roman Catholic Church.

This prayer is taken from *The Interior Castle* and the poetry of Teresa of Ávila. This illustration is based on the cover art by Carole Kowalchuk Odell for the volume on Teresa of Ávila in the Classics of Western Spirituality series by Paulist Press.

FAUSTINA KOWALSKA

Monastic (1905–1938)

Restore us, O God of hosts; let your face shine, that we may be saved.

—*Psalms 80:7*

✠ O my God, my only hope, I have placed all my trust in You and I know I shall not be disappointed,

O Receive us all into the abode of Your Most Compassionate Heart, and never let us escape from It.

✠ Help me, O Lord, that my heart may be merciful so that I may feel all the sufferings of my neighbor.

• I will refuse my heart to no one.

✠ I want to be completely transformed into Your mercy and to be Your living reflection, O Lord.

• May Your unfathomable mercy pass through my heart and soul to my neighbor.

✠ Help me to be merciful, so that I may hurry to assist my neighbor, overcoming my own fatigue and weariness.

• My true rest is in the service of my neighbor.

✠ Eternal God, in whom mercy is endless and the treasury of compassion inexhaustible, look kindly upon us and increase Your mercy in us.

• Divine Mercy, accompanying us every moment of our lives, we Trust in You.

✠ With great confidence we submit ourselves to Your holy will, which is Love and Mercy itself.

O For the sake of His sorrowful Passion have mercy on us and on the whole world.

✠ Jesus, I trust in You.

Almighty and everlasting God, you are always more ready to hear than
we to pray, and to give more than we either desire or deserve: Pour upon
us the abundance of your mercy, forgiving us those things of which our
conscience is afraid, and giving us those good things for which we are
not worthy to ask, except through the merits and mediation of Jesus
Christ our Savior; who lives and reigns with you and the Holy Spirit,
one God, for ever and ever. *Amen.*

From humble beginnings, a poor Polish nun and mystic, Faustina
Kowalska, brought the message of Divine Mercy to the world.

Faustina Kowalska was born in 1905 to devout parents who lived on a farm
near Łódź, Poland. Young Faustina first heard the voice of God calling her to
religious life when she was seven years old. After attending elementary school
for only three years, she worked as a housekeeper to help support her family.
When Faustina's parents denied her request to enter a convent, she turned her
mind to worldly vanities.

In 1924, when Faustina was seventeen, attending a dance at a local park, she
saw a vision of the suffering Christ, who asked her how long she would continue
to ignore his call. She slipped away from the dance to the local cathedral where
she prostrated herself before the Blessed Sacrament, asking guidance for what
she should do next. The Lord told her to go to Warsaw and join a convent. She
returned home, shared her plan with her sister and left on a train for Warsaw
the following morning, bringing nothing but the clothes she was wearing.

Faustina was denied entry to several convents, but finally the Congregation
of Sisters of Our Lady of Mercy told her that she would be allowed entry if she
could purchase a monastic habit. She worked as a housekeeper to save money
before returning a year later to enter the convent. In April 1926, she received

her habit and began her novitiate, working as a lay sister in several convents in
Poland and Lithuania. She experienced a spiritual dark night that persisted for
most of her time as a novice. She made her first profession of temporary vows
in April 1928, which she renewed annually for the next five years.

Although her religious sisters described her as an ordinary nun, Faustina
experienced many extraordinary spiritual gifts and graces, including prophecy,
reading peoples' souls, hidden stigmata, levitation, bilocation, even receiving
Holy Communion from a seraph. After she related her experiences to her spiritual
director, Father Michael Sopocko, he had her undergo psychiatric evaluation as
part of his assessment of the authenticity of her reports. Finally believing them
to be authentic, in 1933 he ordered her to keep a diary of her visions.

In 1931, while she was praying in her cell, she saw the Lord Jesus standing
before her with his right hand raised in a blessing; his left hand touched his
heart, from which emanated two rays, one red and one pale. Jesus told her to
create a painting of this image with the words "Jesus, I trust in you" inscribed
at the bottom. When she told Fr. Sopocko of her vision, he found the artist,
E. Kazimirowski, to paint, under Faustina's guidance, what is now known as
the Divine Mercy Image. Although Faustina cried because the artist could not
capture the true beauty of Jesus, Jesus told her that he wanted the image to be
publicly honored.

Faustina lived with gradually worsening tuberculosis for the last eight
years of her life. During the final two years of her life, as her health declined
significantly, she spent much time in the hospital or sanitorium. During a visit
by Fr. Sopocko, she told him, "My one occupation is to live in the presence of
my Heavenly Father." She died of tuberculosis on October 5, 1938.

Faustina's principal mission was to carry to the world a message that is now
known as The Divine Mercy: that God's love for each of us is greater than any
sin we could commit, that we should let his immeasurable love flow through
us to our neighbor, and that we should entrust God with our lives and our
entire beings. Therefore, we should ask for God's mercy, be merciful to others,
and completely trust in Jesus. Faustina's message has grown into a worldwide

movement that includes five devotional practices, including the Image of Divine Mercy and a Divine Mercy feast day on the Sunday after Easter.

The feast day for Faustina Kowalska in the Roman Catholic Church is October 5.

This prayer was taken from the *Diary of Saint Maria Faustina Kowalska*. The image is taken from a painting of Faustina holding the Divine Mercy Image.

BONAVENTURE

Friar, Cardinal, Theologian,
Doctor of the Church (1217–1274)

Finally, beloved, whatever is true, whatever is honorable, whatever is just, whatever is pure, whatever is pleasing, whatever is commendable, if there is any excellence and if there is anything worthy of praise, think about these things.

—Philippians 4:8

✠ Teach me, O Lord, Your way, that I may walk in Your truth; direct my heart that it may fear Your name.

O The soul, distorted by sin, is reformed by grace; cleansed by righteousness, trained by learning, and perfected by wisdom.

✠ Send us the gift of WISDOM, that we may taste in its life-giving flavor the fruit of the Tree of Life.

• O tree of our salvation, Your fruit is so worthy of desire!

✠ Send us the gift of KNOWLEDGE, that we may be filled with the light of Your sacred teaching to distinguish good from evil.

• Illuminate our minds with your holy light, and instruct us in the ways of humility and love.

✠ Send us the gift of UNDERSTANDING, through which the vision of our mind is clarified.

• O Jesus, You are the way that leads to heaven and the light which illuminates the darkened mind.

✠ Send us the gift of FEAR, that we may draw away from all evil and be kept in peace by the awesome might of Your majesty.

• Teach me, O Lord, Your way; direct my heart that it may fear Your name.

✠ Send us the gift of PIETY that our hearts may be filled with kindness.

O Give us Your Fruit as our food and shed Your light upon our thoughts.

✠ Inspire us with holy thoughts; be unto those who fear Christ a peaceful way of life. *Amen.*

Lord, we pray that your grace may always precede and follow us, that we may continually be given to good works; through Jesus Christ our Lord, who lives and reigns with you and the Holy Spirit, one God, now and for ever. *Amen.*

The writings of Saint Bonaventure combine Franciscan warmth and love of Jesus with the rigorous theology of an academic philosopher—uniting heart and intellect; mysticism and theology; contemplation and action.

Bonaventure, whose name means "Good Things to Come," was born around 1217 in Bagnoregio, Italy, about sixty miles northwest of Rome. When Bonaventure was a boy, he sustained a severe illness that his father, a wealthy physician, was unable to cure. His mother appealed to the intercession of the saintly Francis of Assisi; as Bonaventure later recalled, "I was snatched from the very jaws of death by his intercessions and merits" and "restored to perfect health." "I recognize that God saved my life through him."

When Bonaventure was about seventeen, he was sent to the University of Paris, where he studied under the renowned Franciscan scholar Alexander of Hales; in 1243, he entered the Franciscan Order. Bonaventure earned his license as a bachelor from the university in 1248 and master of theology in about 1253, staying on as a professor to teach. It was in Paris, also, that Bonavenure met the Dominican, Thomas Aquinas, who became his lifelong friend.

Bonaventure's teaching career came to an abrupt halt in 1257, when he was elected minister general of the Franciscan Order, a position he would hold for seventeen years. During his generalate, Bonaventure, an able administrator, brought renewal to the Franciscan Order by remaining faithful to the Franciscan ideals of poverty and simplicity, while adapting the Rule to ensure institutional sustainability. For his adept work in reconciling these two factions, he is often called the second founder of the Franciscan Order.

In the midst of the duties of his term as minister general, Bonaventure found time to write a number of spiritual treatises, sermons, and two biographies of Francis of Assisi. In his early forties, Bonaventure, "seeking peace with a panting spirit," went on a personal retreat to La Verna, the site where Saint Francis received the stigmata from a six-winged seraph in the form of Christ Crucified. While praying, Bonaventure received "all at once" a mystical understanding that he put forth in his major work, *The Mind's Journey Into God*, written in 1259. In this work, he describes a six-stage pathway—one for each wing of the seraph—that symbolizes the spiritual ascent to God through the contemplation of Christ crucified.

In 1273, Pope Gregory X chose Bonaventure to become a cardinal and appointed him bishop of Albano. Bonaventure spent the following year assisting the pope to prepare for the Second Council of Lyons, which aspired, among other things, to unite the Eastern Greek Church with that of the Latin West. During the Council meeting in 1274, Bonaventure died unexpectedly; some have speculated that he was poisoned. He was buried the following day at a service attended by both Greek and Latin clergy, religious and laity, grieving the loss of one of the great thought leaders of the High Middle Ages. He was given the title of "Doctor of the Church," and is called the Seraphic Doctor.

The feast day for Saint Bonaventure is celebrated in the Anglican Communion and the Roman Catholic Church on July 15.

This prayer is taken from *The Journey of the Mind to God*, *The Tree of Life*, and *The Seven Last Words of Christ*. The illustration was inspired by the frontispiece of a 1751 volume of the works of Bonaventure.

ISAAC THE SYRIAN

Poet and Bishop (ca. 640–after 700)

I will give you the treasures of darkness and riches hidden in secret places, so that you may know that it is I, the Lord, *the God of Israel, who call you by your name.*

—Isaiah 45:3

✠ Come, people of discernment, and be filled with wonder!

O May God make us worthy of a taste of His grace, for by it we approach the wonder that surrounds Him.

♦ Taste within yourself Christ's suffering, that you may be deemed worthy of tasting his glory.

• Blessed is the person who has eaten of the Bread of love, which is Jesus.

♦ Without love for our neighbor, the mind is not able to become illuminated by God's divine love.

• God's gift is given to the heart by means of love of one's neighbor.

♦ To entrust oneself to God means no longer being devoured by anguish or fear.

• The person of faith lives constantly in the presence of God.

♦ Bring my will in accordance with your will, for it is you who give prayer to those who pray.

• Turn my heart toward you, cause a hidden light to dwell in me.

♦ At the door of your compassion do I knock, Lord. O Name of Jesus, key to all gifts, open up for me the great door of your treasure house.

O I give praise to your holy Nature, Lord, for you have made my nature a holy temple for your Divinity.

✠ Sanctify me by your mysteries, illumine my mind with knowledge of you, cause your hope to shine forth in my heart, Lord of my life.

Almighty and everlasting God, in Christ you have revealed your glory among the nations: Preserve the works of your mercy, that your Church throughout the world may persevere with steadfast faith in the confession of your Name; through Jesus Christ our Lord, who lives and reigns with you and the Holy Spirit, one God, for ever and ever. *Amen.*

*T*hrough the writing of Isaac the Syrian, we enter with wonder into the glory of the divine and bask in the limitless love and mercy of God.

Isaac's title "the Syrian" does not refer to the country of Syria, but to the Syriac language, a branch of Aramaic, the language spoken by our Lord and others in early Palestine. A unique feature of Syriac Christianity is its remarkable practice of using poetry as an instrument for theological expression.

Isaac was born circa 640 on the western shore of the Persian Gulf, in what is now Qatar, a region then under the jurisdiction of the Syriac Church of Persia.

The two Syriac sources of biographical information on Isaac tell us nothing about his childhood. From his writings, it is clear that Isaac was well educated and was very familiar with Greek writers Evagrius, Macarius, and others. Like many Syriac Christians, he was strongly influenced by the writings of Ephrem of Nisibis (d. 373), whose beautiful hymns and poems were admired for their rich symbolism.

As a young man, Isaac focused on deepening his relationship with Jesus and purifying his own heart. For Isaac, purification was accomplished through daily ascetic practice. He likened the heart to a metal mirror that needed constant polishing in order to render an accurate image; one that could reflect the light of Jesus to the world.

Isaac entered the monastery at Mar Matthew, near Nineveh (near Mosul, Iraq). He was known by his fellow monks for his gentleness, humility, his deep spirituality, and prolific writing. He was also known for his strict asceticism, eating only three loaves of bread and some raw vegetables per week. His brother monks elected him to be their abbot. Around the year 676, Isaac was consecrated Bishop of Nineveh and moved away from the monastery and into the city. At that time, Nineveh was a central site for the East Syrian Nestorian Church, which emphasized the humanity of Christ over his divinity, however there is no evidence that Isaac was a Nestorian.

It appears that Isaac had little interest in church politics and the administrative duties that the bishopric required. He abdicated the episcopacy of Nineveh after only five months, "for a reason which only God knows," according to one biographer, preferring to return to life as a solitary.

Isaac retired to "the desert," which in his case meant the mountainous region of what is now southeastern Iraq. There he continued his ascetic practices, living as a solitary in a nearby cell, returning to the monastery of Rabban Shabur for Saturday night rituals, Sunday liturgy, and to receive a portion of food for the coming week. As an elder, Isaac's failing eyesight required that younger monks read to him and take dictation, allowing him to transmit his spiritual wisdom to future generations. He died at "an old age."

Isaac's writings were not initially embraced by the Church due to fears of influence by the Nestorians in Nineveh. However, the spiritual depth and richness of his work transcended these concerns, and he is now one of the most widely read spiritual writers in Eastern Orthodoxy.

The feast day for Isaac the Syrian in the Eastern Orthodox Church and the Roman Catholic Church is January 28.

This prayer is taken from his homilies on the inner life. The illustration is based on contemporary icons written by Teodor Zinon and Baker Galloway.

Sunday Closest to October 19—Proper 24

PAULI MURRAY

Lawyer, Poet, Priest (1910–1985)

The Lord *said to him, "This is the land of which I swore to Abraham, to Isaac, and to Jacob, saying, 'I will give it to your descendants'; I have let you see it with your eyes, but you shall not cross over there."*

—*Deut. 34:4*

✝ Eternal God, so mightily spread abroad your Spirit, that all peoples may be gathered under the banner of the Prince of Peace.

O In Jesus Christ we have a vision of our higher destiny; Christ goes before us pointing the way.

✠ Jesus made our actions toward strangers and outcasts the test of our love of God.

• Give me a song of kindliness, and a country where I can live it.

✠ It is only when we are one in Christ that we can rise above those things that separate us from one another.

• Give me a song of hope and a world where I can sing it.

✠ Faith teaches us that God's Spirit is with us continually in our pain and brokenness, reconciling us and the world to himself.

• Give me a song of faith and a people to believe in it.

✠ In this faith we can be hopeful amid the uncertainties of the world, and we can be joyful, even in the midst of sorrow and pain.

• Give me a song of hope and love, and a brown girl's heart to hear it.

✠ O God, give us the courage and faith to go on, to carry our share of the burden through to the end.

O Whatever the pain and cost, it is through the discipline of forgiveness that we are healed and become more whole.

✝ The light of God's eternal love shines in the darkness, and we shall be safe.

Almighty and everlasting God, increase in us the gifts of faith, hope, and charity; and, that we may obtain what you promise, make us love what you command; through Jesus Christ our Lord, who lives and reigns with you and the Holy Spirit, one God, for ever and ever. *Amen.*

*P*auli Murray was one of the most influential advocates for social justice in the United States in the twentieth century, coupling the principles of nonviolence to innovative legal strategies to fight racial and gender-based discrimination.

Born in Baltimore, Maryland, in 1910, Pauli was adopted by her aunt Pauline after her mother died unexpectedly when Pauli was three years old. Pauline raised her niece at the family homestead in Durham, North Carolina, where they lived with Pauli's maternal grandparents and her aunt Sallie. Young Pauli, an avid reader, frequently read the Bible to her elderly grandmother, who took special delight in the Psalms.

After graduating from Hunter College in 1933, Pauli worked odd jobs before applying to graduate school at the University of North Carolina, where she was refused admittance on racial grounds. She worked for the Workers Defense League to raise funds for Odell Waller. This experience led her to apply to the Howard University School of Law, where in 1944, she would become its first woman graduate. Although she was the top student in her class, she was refused admittance for graduate studies at Harvard University because she was a woman.

Pauli's wrote the groundbreaking legal publication, *States' Laws on Race and Color* for the Board of Missions of the Methodist Church in 1951, considered the "bible" of the early efforts to overturn the "separate but equal" doctrine that upheld racial segregation. Other legal papers that Pauli wrote were instrumental in influencing Supreme Court decisions that eventually forbade discrimination based on race or gender.

After many brushes with discriminatory hiring practices, Pauli landed a job with a prestigious New York law firm in 1956. It was there that she met Renee Barlow, the firm's personnel director and a fellow Episcopalian, with whom she would form a lifelong partnership. During the tumultuous 1960s, Pauli served as a professor of law at the University of Ghana, was appointed by John F. Kennedy to the Presidential Commission on the Status of Women, became the first Black student to receive a JSD degree from Yale University, cofounded the National Organization of Women, and taught at Benedict College and Brandeis University.

Pauli's trailblazing life was marked with both trial and triumph. Her numerous groundbreaking accomplishments were achieved against a backdrop of struggle. In addition to battling racism and sexism, Pauli struggled with her gender identity, acknowledging both male and female aspects of her persona, and she regarded Renee Barlow as her "life partner." These many conflicts contributed to her struggle with mental health that resulted in numerous hospitalizations.

In 1968, Pauli was invited to participate in the Assembly of the World Council of Churches, in Uppsala, Sweden, where she helped draft a statement on racism and served on the women's caucus. Her work at the conference inspired Pauli to strive to remove all barriers to full participation in Christ's ministry of reconciliation. Following the death of her partner Renee Barlow in 1973, Pauli felt called to the ordained ministry. At the age of sixty-two, she entered the General Theological Seminary and served as a seminarian at the same chapel in southern Maryland where her uncle had been a vicar.

Pauli was ordained as an Episcopal priest in 1977, becoming the Church's first Black woman priest. Following her ordination, she celebrated her first Holy Eucharist in North Carolina at the same church where her grandmother, an enslaved woman, had been baptized in 1854. Though she officially retired at age seventy-two, as required by Church law, Pauli continued serving in a ministry of reconciliation until her death in 1985.

Sunday Closest to October 26—Proper 25

Pauli Murray is commemorated in the Episcopal Church on July 1.

The words for this prayer are taken from Pauli Murray's sermons and from Pauli's poem "Dark Testament." The illustration was inspired by an icon written by Zach Rosemann for the General Theological Seminary.

TERESA OF KOLKATA

Monastic (1910–1997)

The greatest among you will be your servant. All who exalt themselves will be humbled, and all who humble themselves will be exalted."

—*Matthew 23:11–12*

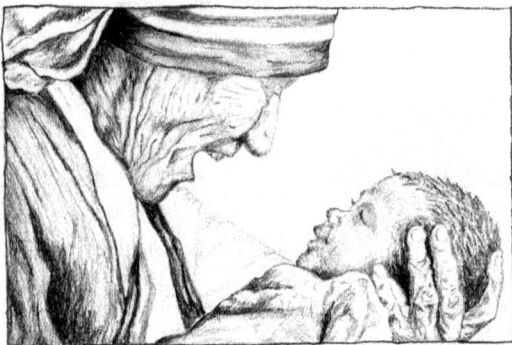

✠ Dear Lord, help me to understand now what wholehearted service means.

O We cannot love nor serve unless we learn to ponder in our hearts.

✠ In the silence of the heart God speaks; let God fill us, then only we speak.

• Silence is the root of our union with God and with one another.

✠ The fruit of silence is prayer. The fruit of prayer is faith. The fruit of faith is love.

• Love, to be true, has to begin with God in prayer.

✠ The fruit of love is service. The fruit of service is peace.

• Be the fruit of Christ's love in the world.

✠ Dear Jesus, It's you shining on others through me.

• Come, be my light, be my fire of God.

✠ Never separate Jesus in the Eucharist and Jesus in the poor. Externally you see just bread, but it is Jesus. Externally you see just the poor person, but it is Jesus.

O May you grow in that holiness for which Our Lord has created you.

✠ My God, give us courage now—this moment—to persevere in following Your call.

Almighty and merciful God, it is only by your gift that your faithful people offer you true and laudable service: Grant that we may run without stumbling to obtain your heavenly promises; through Jesus Christ our Lord, who lives and reigns with you and the Holy Spirit, one God, now and for ever. *Amen.*

*M*other Teresa encountered Jesus by serving the "poorest of the poor" and remaining true to her faith, despite suffering decades of profound spiritual aridity.

Mother Teresa, as she was known to the world, was born in Skopje, now located in North Macedonia, in 1910. Her parents were ethnic Albanians who raised her in the faith. After her father's death when Teresa was eight, her family struggled economically, but her mother often shared what little food they had with neighbors who had less. Teresa first discerned a religious vocation at age twelve, showing a keen interest in foreign missions. After six years of prayer, Teresa responded to this call by joining the Loreto Sisters and embarking to Dublin, Ireland, in October 1928 at the age of eighteen.

After six weeks of training in Ireland, Teresa set sail for India, arriving on the Feast of the Epiphany 1929. She officially began her novitiate in May and began two years of intense training and formation, making her temporary vows in 1931 and her final profession in 1937. Mother Teresa taught at the convent school in Darjeeling, becoming its principal in 1944; she would remain with the Loreto Sisters for twenty years.

In 1946, when Mother Teresa was returning to Darjeeling by train from her annual retreat, she received what she described as a "call within a call" from God to dedicate her life to caring for "the poorest of the poor" in the slums of Kolkata. In subsequent locutions, Jesus spoke to her directly, asking her to undertake this mission for him. Her call was tested for two years by her confessor and her archbishop before she finally received approval from Rome to start a new religious congregation. Mother Teresa received basic training in nursing care and began serving Jesus by caring for people in need; soon, former students joined her efforts. "Not all of us can do great things," she was fond of saying, "but we can do small things with great love."

The new community, the Missionaries of Charity, which would become known around the world by their white saris edged with blue borders, was officially established in 1950. Mother Teresa persuaded city authorities to provide a building to serve as a hospice; she also opened a home for children, schools, and distribution centers for food and medical aid. By the early 1960s the order had spread throughout India, and in 1964 they opened their first house in Venezuela. As of 2025, there were more than 5,500 Missionaries of Charity serving in nearly 140 countries; the organization now includes active and contemplative branches for men, priests, and laity.

As the organization expanded, it attracted the attention of foreign media, which Mother Teresa used adeptly to further her mission. During the 1960s and 1970s, she met with the Pope and world leaders, including Queen Elizabeth II and two US presidents. She received numerous prestigious awards, culminating with the award of the Nobel Peace Prize in 1979, which she received "for the glory of God and in the name of the poor."

In the 1980s Mother Teresa's health declined, and she experienced a heart attack in 1989. The following year she tried to resign as head of the order, but her resignation was rejected by the members. As her heart condition worsened, the order eventually chose the India-born Sister Nirmala as her successor. Mother Teresa's earthly life ended in 1997.

The publication of Mother Teresa's private letters after her death revealed that for the last fifty years of her life, she experienced a deep spiritual darkness, feeling unloved and unwanted by God. In spite of the great anguish this caused her, her love of Jesus was undiminished. "Never let anything so fill you with sorrow as to make you forget the joy of the Risen Christ," she said.

Sunday Closest to November 2—Proper 26

Mother Teresa is celebrated in the Anglican Communion and by the Roman Catholic Church on September 5.

This prayer is based on the letters of Mother Teresa to her spiritual advisors and to the Missionaries of Charity. The drawing is based on a photograph by E. Adams published in the *New York Times*.

C. S. LEWIS

Apologist and Spiritual Writer (1898–1963)

Give ear, O my people, to my teaching; incline your ears to the words of my mouth.
I will open my mouth in a parable; I will utter dark sayings from of old, things that
we have heard and known, that our ancestors have told us.

—Psalms 78:1–3

✢ Into the void of silence, into the empty space of nothing, the joy of life is unfurled.

O Joy bursts in our lives when we go about doing the good at hand and not trying to manipulate things to achieve joy.

✤ God does not love us because we are good, but God makes us good because He loves us.

• I cannot learn to love God except by learning to obey Him.

✤ I cannot learn to love my neighbor as myself until I learn to love God.

• Love is a steady wish for the loved person's ultimate good.

✤ In self-giving, we touch a rhythm not only of all creation but of all being.

• The instrument through which you see God is your whole self.

✤ The soul's union with God is a continual self-abandonment—an opening, an unveiling, a surrender, of itself.

• Each soul will be eternally engaged in giving away that which it receives.

✤ Those who are united with God in eternity share His splendor and power and joy.

O There is no neutral ground in the universe: every square inch, every split second, is claimed by God and counterclaimed by Satan.

✢ Now, today, this moment, is our chance to choose the right. We must take it or leave it.

O God, whose blessed Son came into the world that he might destroy the works of the devil and make us children of God and heirs of eternal life: Grant that, having this hope, we may purify ourselves as he is pure; that, when he comes again with power and great glory, we may be made like him in his eternal and glorious kingdom; where he lives and reigns with you and the Holy Spirit, one God, for ever and ever. *Amen.*

C. S. Lewis used his penetrating prose and imaginative storytelling to help us see the truth of the Gospel.

Clive Staples Lewis, was born in 1898 in Belfast, Ireland, to a middle-class family. Lewis and his brother Warnie grew up in a house full of books and learned to read by the age of three. His childhood was shattered by his mother's death when he was nine, after which Lewis was sent away to English boarding schools, which he despised. A private tutor later schooled him in the classics and critical thinking, but disabused him of whatever faith he had in God, and Lewis became an avowed atheist.

In April 1917, Lewis began studies at University College, Oxford, but enlisted in the British infantry before completing his first year. He served in the trenches of the Somme Valley in France, but returned to England after he was wounded by shrapnel. Lewis honored his promise to Paddy Moore, who was killed in the Great War, to take care of his family; he lived with Paddy's mother and sister from 1921 onward. After Lewis's father died in 1929, he and his brother Warnie combined their inheritance with funds from Mrs. Moore to purchase an eight-acre property near Oxford, known as The Kilns.

Lewis completed his studies at Oxford, earning three First-Class Honours in Classical Literature, Philosophy, and English Literature. Lewis then stayed on at Oxford as a tutor in English literature and was elected a fellow of Magdalen

College in 1925, a position he held for twenty-nine years. In 1926, Lewis met the writer J. R. R. Tolkien, a devout Roman Catholic, who was also on the English faculty at Oxford. As their friendship grew, Lewis's thoughts about God began to change until he finally admitted in 1930 "that God was God." He began praying and attending chapel, though at this time he described himself as a theist and did not believe in the divinity of Christ. It was not until September 1931 that Lewis's conversion was complete. Conversations with Tolkien and Hugo Dyson helped Lewis to see Christianity as "a true myth" that "really happened," a union of imagination and reason. In 1933 the three men became core members of the Inklings, a literary group that bonded over literature and alcohol.

Lewis felt duty bound to bring the Christian message to a wider audience and began writing articles for the newspaper, delivering radio talks for the BBC, and speaking publicly about his faith. These widely popular (though academically disdained) efforts were later published in book format as *The Problem of Pain, The Screwtape Letters,* and *Mere Christianity.* Over his lifetime, C. S. Lewis wrote more than thirty books.

Many have come to know C. S. Lewis through the *Chronicles of Narnia,* his richly imaginative seven-volume series that tells the adventures of four children who enter a portal into a mythical realm. These allegorical stories allow readers to *feel* what God is like and to inhabit the Christian narrative in an experiential way that is not accessible through his strictly theological works, such as *Mere Christianity,* though they deal with many of the same themes. Five of the books were written between 1948 and 1951, with the final two volumes completed in 1952 and 1954; the books were published between 1950 and 1956.

In 1955 Lewis began a new position teaching Medieval and Renaissance Literature at Magdalen College, Cambridge, spending weekdays in Cambridge, and returning to The Kilns on weekends. When Lewis was fifty-eight, he married Joy Davidman, an American poet, to prevent her from being deported to the United States. Although initially their marriage was one of convenience, they grew to love each other deeply, and her death in 1960 devastated Lewis. In *A Grief Observed,* he shared his anger at God and revealed how his faith helped transform his grief into gratitude for the love that they shared together. Lewis died later at The Kilns in 1963.

C. S. Lewis is commemorated by the Anglican Communion on November 22 or on November 29.

This prayer was taken from the apologetic writings of C. S. Lewis. The drawing is based on a photo of C. S. Lewis taken in 1951 by Arthur Strong.

JEROME

Monastic, Priest, and Scholar (ca. 342/7–420)

So teach us to count our days, that we may gain a wise heart.

—Psalms 90:12

✠ Let us pray to the Lord that we may become as fire, so that we may grow warm with the Holy Spirit.

O The grace of the Holy Spirit is found in the river of the Sacred Scriptures.

✠ Make knowledge of Scripture your love; make them the sole object of your knowledge and love.

• If you do not know the Scriptures, you do not know Christ.

✠ The soul with the knowledge of Scripture is the dwelling place of God.

• We are ascending upward gradually to a mystical understanding.

✠ For those who follow the Word of God and ascend the mountain, for them, Jesus is instantly transfigured.

• Holy Scripture directs my steps, lest I stumble.

✠ If one does not feed on the Word of God, one does not live.

• Sacred Scripture is the food for the soul.

✠ The divine Word is exceedingly rich, containing within itself every delight.

O Let us read Sacred Scripture, and day and night, let us ponder over its every syllable and every letter.

✠ Let us beg the Lord that everything that we have said we may translate words into works.

Blessed Lord, who caused all holy Scriptures to be written for our learning: Grant us so to hear them, read, mark, learn, and inwardly digest them, that we may embrace and ever hold fast the blessed hope of everlasting life, which you have given us in our Savior Jesus Christ; who lives and reigns with you and the Holy Spirit, one God, for ever and ever. *Amen.*

*S*aint Jerome invites us to a deeper personal relationship with God through study of the Holy Scriptures.

Jerome was born in Stridon, Dalmatia, probably in coastal Slovenia or Croatia, around the year 347. His wealthy Christian family provided him with an excellent education, sending him to Rome when he was about twelve years old. There he studied grammar, rhetoric, philosophy, and Latin literature, though, by his later admission, he neglected his religious education.

In 366, when Jerome was about nineteen years old, he was baptized by Pope Liberius. After completing his formal education, he traveled in Italy, Gaul, and back to Dalmatia. In Trier, he experienced a religious conversion and decided to become a monk. From there he went to Aquileia, Italy, where he lived in a small community of like-minded Christians.

After three years, Jerome removed to Syrian Antioch, where he deepened his knowledge of Greek. During Lent 375, he had a life-changing dream in which he came before a heavenly tribunal which found him guilty of preferring pagan literature to the Holy Scriptures. "You are a Ciceronian, not a Christian; for where your treasure is, there also is your heart," Christ proclaimed. Upon waking from the dream, Jerome vowed never to read pagan literature again and left for the desert of Chalcis, where he lived a rigorously ascetic life, immersing himself in Holy Scripture, "with none but the scorpions and wild beasts for companions." To combat temptations of hermetic life, Jerome began learning Hebrew from a Jew who had converted to Christianity and become a monk.

Before leaving Syria, Jerome was reluctantly ordained a priest. He then traveled to Constantinople, where he studied Scripture with Gregory Nazianzus and wrote his first biblical commentary. In 382, Jerome accompanied Paulinus to Rome to serve as his translator. While there, he was asked by Pope Damasus to serve as an advisor and secretary. The Pope then asked Jerome to embark on a new translation of the Bible, based on the original texts. While in Rome, he completed translations of the Psalms and New Testament. Jerome would work on this project, eventually called "the Vulgate," i.e., the "common language" version of the Bible, for more than three decades.

While he was in Rome, Jerome became the spiritual advisor to a group of noblewomen. From the more than forty extant letters to the women, it is clear that Jerome recognized women as his colleagues and equals in scholarship, asceticism, and religious life, serving as a teacher and mentor for Saint Paula of Rome, her daughter Saint Eustochium, Saint Marcella, and others.

After the Pope's death in 384, Jerome left Rome, finally settling in Bethlehem, where he was joined by Paula and Eustochium. With generous financial support from Paula, they established a monastery, three communities for women, and a hospice for pilgrims. Jerome resumed his hermetic lifestyle, taking residence in a cave near the Grotto of the Nativity. From this cell, Jerome continued his translation of the Old Testament. He remained in Bethlehem until his death in 420.

Saint Jerome is celebrated throughout the Church on September 30 in the West and on June 15 in the East.

This prayer is taken from Saint Jerome's *Homilies* on the Psalms and his *Commentary on Galatians*. The illustration is based on the frontispiece of a 1492 publication of the letters of Saint Jerome from the British Library archive.

THOMAS MERTON

Monastic, Mystic, Priest, Social Reformer

(1915–1968)

Make a joyful noise to the Lord, all the earth. Worship the Lord *with gladness; come into his presence with singing.*

—*Psalms 100:1*

✠ O God, teach us to be content with Your grace that comes to us in darkness and that works things we cannot see.

O By grace we are able to share in the infinitely selfless love of Christ.

✠ Do not think that you can show your love for Christ by hating those who seem to be His enemies on earth. He loves them, and you cannot be united with Him unless you love them too.

• Our job is to love others without stopping to inquire whether or not they are worthy.

✠ When the Love of God is in me, God is able to love you through me.

• We seek unity because we are the image of the One God.

✠ We are already one. But we imagine we are not. And what we have to recover is our original unity.

• When we are one with God's love, we own all things in Him.

✠ We are members one of another and everything that is given to one member is given for the whole body.

• Every breath we draw is a gift of God's love; every moment of existence is a grace.

✠ When we love God's will we find Him and own His joy in all things.

O Love is our true destiny. We do not find the meaning of life by ourselves alone. We find it with one another.

✠ May we all grow in grace and peace and not neglect the silence that is printed in the center of our being. It will not fail us.

Almighty and everlasting God, whose will it is to restore all things in your well-beloved Son, the King of kings and Lord of lords: Mercifully grant that the peoples of the earth, divided and enslaved by sin, may be freed and brought together under his most gracious rule; who lives and reigns with you and the Holy Spirit, one God, now and for ever. *Amen.*

In silence and solitude Thomas Merton learned to hear the voice of God; his writing shared this mystery with the world.

Thomas Merton was born in the French Pyrenees in 1915; his father, an Anglican from New Zealand, and his mother, an American Quaker, were both painters. His childhood was one of sadness and instability, marred by the deaths of his mother when he was six and his father when he was fifteen. He had a peripatetic youth, attending boarding schools in France and England, and living with relatives in the United States and abroad.

Shortly after his eighteenth birthday, Thomas went to Italy, where he was captivated by the beauty of the Italian churches; he purchased a Vulgate Bible and, for the first time in his life, began to pray. The following fall, he attended Clare College, Cambridge, where he lived a debauched life of "wenching and drinking," as he later described it. Thomas fathered a child out of wedlock, his grades fell, and he lost his scholarship.

In 1935 Thomas returned to New York to live with his grandparents and attended Colombia University, where he received BA and MA degrees in English. His conversion to Christianity occurred largely through reading, most notably, the works of Gerald Manley Hopkins, William Blake, Étienne Gilson, and Aldous Huxley. He began attending Mass, and in 1938, after reading a biography of Hopkins, Thomas made the decision to seek Holy Baptism, receiving the Sacrament and First Communion in November 1938.

Sunday Closest to November 23—Proper 29

During Easter week 1939, Thomas visited Cuba, where he experienced the presence of God during Mass, transforming his faith from an intellectual understanding to a profoundly joyful and heartfelt belief. In 1940, he took a teaching position at St. Bonaventure College, continuing to deepen his prayer life, and he began exploring a religious vocation. Deeply disappointed when the Franciscans did not accept him as a candidate, Thomas attended a retreat at the Our Lady of Gethsemani Abbey in Kentucky, which accepted him as a postulant the following year, when he was twenty-seven. This Trappist monastery would be his home for the remainder of his life.

Thomas published his first volume of poems in 1944, the year he made his simple vow. As his gift for writing became known, his abbot ordered him to write his autobiography, which was published in 1948 as *The Seven Storey Mountain* and became a *New York Times* bestseller. The following year he was ordained a priest. Thomas would publish more than fifty books over the next twenty-seven years.

In 1958, after seventeen years of living as a monk, Thomas experienced a life-changing epiphany while standing in downtown Louisville, Kentucky, on the corner of Fourth and Walnut streets. Looking at the people rushing about, he had the sudden "realization that I loved all those people, that they were mine and I theirs." He saw that each of us "is like a pure diamond, blazing with the invisible light of heaven." This realization fueled his later peace advocacy and his desire to learn from other religious traditions. "The gate of Heaven is everywhere," he believed.

Thomas was a proponent of interfaith dialogue, developing friendships with Thich Nhat Hanh, D. T. Suzuki, and Dalai Lama Tenzin Gyatso, seeking to discover common threads of monasticism across religions. In 1968 he received permission to travel to Asia, hoping to "drink from ancient sources of monastic vision," to deepen his own contemplative practice. He died while in Thailand attending an international meeting of Catholic abbots, where he was a keynote speaker. His death has been attributed to accidental electrocution from a faulty electric fan, though many questions about his death remain unanswered.

Sunday Closest to November 23—Proper 29

Thomas Merton is commemorated in the Anglican Communion on December 10.

This prayer is taken from *New Seeds of Contemplation, Thoughts in Solitude,* and other writings. The illustration is based on an undated photograph of Thomas Merton in his hermitage and artwork by Julie Lonneman.

NEXT STEPS

id you have a favorite saint? If you enjoyed getting to know these saints, I invite you to take your relationship to the next level. Here are some things you might enjoy:

Celebrate your favorite saint's feast or commemoration day. Eat their food, listen to their music, look at their art. Sing their songs. In chapter fourteen of his *Holy Rule,* Saint Benedict instructs his monks to celebrate the anniversaries of the saints.

If you don't have one already, adopt a patron saint and ask for their special intercession. It could be a saint that shares your first name, or a saint with particular patronage for a favorite activity. Or even a saint that you especially admire. Learn more about them—read their *vita* or a more recent biography. Mark their feast day or commemoration day on your calendar and celebrate it each year. Pray to them.

Buy (or paint!) an icon of your favorite saint. There are so many artists whose work is available online. A few of them offer online classes in which you can learn about the symbolism and techniques of iconography. Some of my favorite contemporary iconographers are: Christine Hales, Ben Lansing, Kelly Latimore, Br. Robert Lentz, Julie Lonneman, and Lewis Williams . . . just to name a few.

Buy a statue or medal depicting the saint. Dorothy Day kept a small statue of Saint Joan of Arc beside her bed. Or make your own prayer beads with the saint's medal at the end of the pendant.

Pay attention to depictions of saints. Go to an art museum and look for saints; go into churches and pay attention to the stained glass windows—they are often full of depictions of saints.

Listen to music written by or about saints—there are many superb recordings of the ethereal music of Hildegard; there are odes, chants, and cantatas written in praise of the saints. Feel free to sing along!

Watch a movie or video about your favorite saint. Full-length feature films or documentaries have been made about most of the saints in this book. Even Polycarp has a movie about him. There are also some great YouTube channels that produce animated biographies of the saints for children (but I like them, too).

Plan a pilgrimage or add a day (or even a few hours) of pilgrimage to your next vacation by visiting a site of significance in the lives of one of the saints. Or visit a church named after your favorite saint; go inside, light a candle, and say a prayer. For example, if you are in downtown Louisville, Kentucky, you may want to visit the "corner of Fourth and Walnut" where a historical marker commemorates Thomas Merton's epiphany—possibly the only historical marker in the United States marking a mystical experience. In fact, there are a surprising number of historical markers commemorating the lives of the saints. Look them up at https://www.hmdb.org/.

And, of course, read their biographies, autobiographies, and writings. Once you've explored their writings in greater depth, write your own prayer. If there are saints who particularly inspired you, create your own novena practice by setting a prayerful intention and reciting that saint's prayer for nine days; the nine days that proceed their feast or commemoration is a particularly auspicious time for a novena.

The saints are alive in Christ. Be open to the experience of their lives intertwining with ours. Let them help you grow closer to Christ. Find a saint whose life and words resonate with you and invite them into your life.

ACKNOWLEDGMENTS

Many thanks to those who have provided feedback on various iterations of the manuscript, especially Marie-Jeanne Verhassel, Lorin Stieff, Susanne Methven, Jan Fuller, and Sarah Bartenstein.

I am grateful to my daughter Caroline, without whose encouragement, I never would have undertaken the illustrations.

Special thanks to all who have provided moral support throughout the writing process, especially Susan Leonard, Betty Wade Perry, Gabriel Gotschall and the people of Saint Nathaniel's Episcopal Church.

I am indebted to the team at Church Publishing for their expertise, especially Roma Maitlall, Mark Powers, Anne Zaccardelli, Amiri Taylor-Barksdale, Andy Berry, Phil Marino, and Eve Strillacci.

Finally, I give thanks to Saint Benedict and all the saints whose words and guidance continue to be an inspiration.

www.ingramcontent.com/pod-product-compliance
Lightning Source LLC
Chambersburg PA
CBHW060045100426
42742CB00014B/2699